MOTHERHOOD:
WHAT IT DOES TO
YOUR MIND

Jane Price, MBBS MRCPsyche., is a psychiatrist and psychotherapist in the National Health Service. She trained at St Bartholomew's before taking up positions in Southampton and Nottingham; she is currently Consultant Psychotherapist to Berkshire, where she specialises in the psychology of women. Jane Price is married and has two sons.

ISSUES IN WOMEN'S HEALTH

Series editor: Sheila Kitzinger

Pandora is publishing an international series of investigative, informative and jargon-free books written by women about all aspects of our bodies and our health.

Especially commissioned and introduced by Sheila Kitzinger, each takes into account women's lives in different countries and cultures, and challenges conventional assumptions about health issues which affect us all.

The first books in this series are:

The Midwife Challenge edited by Sheila Kitzinger
The Tentative Pregnancy: Prenatal Diagnosis and the Future of Motherhood by Barbara Katz Rothman
The Politics of Breastfeeding by Gabrielle Palmer
Motherhood: What It Does To Your Mind by Jane Price

Forthcoming books will cover fat women and the dieting industry, cancer, surrogate motherhood, contraception and fertility, and reproductive technologies.

See back of book for further details and other Pandora health books.

MOTHERHOOD
WHAT IT DOES TO YOUR MIND

JANE PRICE

PANDORA

LONDON   SYDNEY   WELLINGTON

First published by Pandora Press, an imprint of
Unwin Hyman, 1988

Pandora Press
Unwin Hyman Limited
15–17 Broadwick Street, London W1V 1FP

Allen and Unwin Australia Pty Ltd
8 Napier Street, North Sydney, NSW 2060, Australia

Allen and Unwin New Zealand Pty Ltd
 with the Port Nicholson Press,
60 Cambridge Terrace, Wellington, New Zealand

British Library Cataloguing in Publication Data

Price, Jane
  Motherhood: what it does to your mind.
1. Motherhood. Psychological aspects
I. Title
155.6′ 463
ISBN 0–86358–211–7

Set in 10 on 11 point Trump by Grove Graphics, Tring, Herts
and printed in Great Britain by Cox & Wyman Ltd, Reading

CONTENTS

FOREWORD

Depression, anxiety, numbing exhaustion, pervading guilt and a shattering loss of self-esteem are occupational hazards of being a mother in industrial cultures. The switchback of emotional highs and lows on which a mother finds herself, the sense of being imprisoned with an enemy alien, and the self-hatred and horror that you could have such terrible thoughts about your adored, much-loved child – all these are often attributed to a new mother's disturbed endocrine system. Women are told that it is all due to hormones and the implication is that they cannot help but be victims of their bodies.

To believe this is to become further disempowered. Just as girls used to be told that they were 'unwell' when they menstruated and that they must not wash their hair or exert themselves then, and as women expected to become old with the menopause, women are forced to explain the distress they experience at the way in which society is treating them by reference to their glands. In this way many of the major psycho-physical processes in women's lives serve to further tighten around them the straitjacket constructed by spurious biological theories.

In this book a feminist psychiatrist, who has herself survived motherhood, explores how modern culture treats mothers, ways in which the work of being a mother is trivialised and degraded, and how, even if women manage to continue to function 'normally', it is difficult for us to retain any self-confidence.

She points to the kind of rethinking we need to do in order to understand ourselves as mothers, and at ways in which we need to change our society. The book makes a provocative, stimulating, challenging read.

Sheila Kitzinger
Oxford, 1988

ACKNOWLEDGMENTS

I would like to thank the many women who have shared their experiences as mothers with me over the years. These women include friends and relatives as well as patients. I would also like to thank the nannies, mothers' helps and au pairs without whom my chosen lifestyle would have been impossible. Knowing these women, being encouraged and supported by them and being allowed to share in their experiences as they have shared in mine has been a great privilege.

I would like to add my heartfelt thanks for the support of my parents.

A number of colleagues have given support and helpful criticism of the finished product, and many have contributed to my knowledge and understanding over the years. My thanks to them and to my patient secretary, Michelle Dunkley for much photocopying and general help.

Finally, my thanks to Ben and Sam for supporting this project even when it meant I had less time for them and to Farouk, my husband. I have always thought I would be impressed to find a book written by a woman who thanks her husband for typing the manuscript. He did the next best thing in buying my word processor.

1

INTRODUCTION

Everyone has an image of and some basic assumptions about what a mother is. We have all experienced being mothered in some form or another, and we have complex feelings about that experience, some of which we could discuss openly but some of which are hidden, even from ourselves, in the darkest recesses of our minds. The way in which we judge or accept our own mothers colours the way in which we are likely to perceive ourselves and others as parents. What we say about mothering may not truly reflect what we feel. What we believe ourselves to feel may only be part of what is buried in the unconscious area of the mind. Becoming a mother often challenges and then alters these images and the assumptions.

Our psychological lives are complex and, for the most part, rather mysterious. The thinking, rational part of our mind, the conscious mind, is available to us openly. We know what we think, we can summon memories and experiences, we can hold conversations and relate to others with this part of our mind and feel in control of what we are doing or saying. Beneath this controlled exterior lurk two more layers of psychological functioning however. The first of these layers is the semi-conscious. In that part of our mind is the information we can only half remember, the things we say that are slips of the tongue and the actions we take that we can only half understand. It is not that such things are actively buried in our minds but rather that there is a limit to the amount of information the conscious mind can carry at any one time and the semi-conscious functions as a storehouse for other information, so that it can be readily available when we need it. Underneath this storehouse is another much vaster reservoir of information which is not readily available to us, although capable of influencing our every thought, word or action. This is called the unconscious.

The unconscious part of our mind is like a deep pool from whose depths things can rise to the surface unexpectedly. We lay down memories from our earliest moments, even before we can use words to help us structure our thoughts. These memories are of emotions and experiences that stretch back to the beginnings of our brains *in utero*. Most of us cannot remember our lives consciously before the age of 3 or 4. A small number can remember back to the age of 1, but very few before that. Many cannot remember anything until they were 7 or 8. Obviously then, we each existed for a period of time about which we know nothing consciously. We experienced the dependency of a small baby, the rage of being frustrated and helpless, the sadness of discovering our mothers were not part of us, and not perfect either, and stored all those experiences and their accompanying emotions away in our unconscious minds before we started on the part of our childhood that we can easily 'remember'.

An important part of what we experienced and then stored away out of sight consisted of the parenting we received as babies. Children often question their mothers for information about their childhood, wanting to hear again and again the stories about their births for instance, as if trying to recapture in their developing conscious minds the experiences that are already out of reach. None of us can claim to consciously know what transpired between our mothers and ourselves in those early years. If we do have information about events and feelings it will be second-hand, either from our mothers or other close relatives or friends, and it will be information from an adult perspective, almost certainly coloured by how the adult wanted to perceive the relationship. What we cannot remember is not totally lost to us however. In the earliest days of our experience we are laying down the basic assumptions about ourselves and others that will guide our lives and relationships throughout adulthood. This template survives as a testimony to our individual and unique experience. It is a template that is formed of the material we inherited from our parents, but strongly patterned by those early experiences about which we consciously know so little.

One of the strongest patterns on the template is etched by our experience of being parented, probably by being mothered as fathers tend to be more distant figures in a baby's young life. Hence our basic assumptions and expectations of mothering rise out of that unknown pool of knowledge that lies within us and yet outside of our influence. So deeply etched and then buried are these assumptions that it takes a personal earthquake to question or change them. For many, becoming a parent themselves is that earthquake.

Our conscious expectations of mothering may be very different from the basic assumptions that lurk in the unconscious. Women who have had disastrous experiences with their own mothers may well bury any memory of those problems and believe themselves to be good friends with their mothers in adulthood. Their mothers too may have 'forgotten' the problems they experienced as young mothers years before they become grandparents.

The extent of this 'forgetting' is extraordinary and particularly so for events and experiences that were painful and overwhelming for the participants. For several years I was the therapist of a young woman who had had a stillborn son some time before we met. She had coped very adequately with this tragedy until, some six months after the stillbirth, her mother had verbally attacked her for being a wicked and malignant mother to the dead child. This attack made little sense in the content of what the participants remembered. However, after months of exploration it became clear that the woman had been one of twins, the other of which, a boy, had been a stillbirth. Her mother had 'forgotten' this fact for many years and alongside of the memory she had also buried her irrational but deeply held feelings that her daughter had killed her son *in utero* and was therefore responsible for both her mother's and now her own loss. Although my client had never had any conscious suspicions about her birth prior to her father revealing the truth, she was aware that throughout her childhood her mother had treated her with considerable hardness and had always favoured her younger brother. She had also referred during therapy, on a number of occasions, to a sense of something or someone missing from her life, a feeling she had hoped to cure by having a child of her own. The entire family had 'forgotten' this event even though it coloured all their relationships until the second stillbirth reawakened memories. The memories did not come back in a flash, but rather rose like a mist from each of their unconscious minds in turn to complete the sad picture.

Most mothers forget a great deal of what they experience as mothers to young children. Hence the story they tell to their children is a psychologically vetted version of the real event. Mothers who resent the pain of childbirth and blame the child for it, may, for instance, make the story of the birth into an awful ordeal that leaves the child feeling guilty and to blame for everything that distresses its mother. One patient described this to me as 'having wounded my mother body and soul. I felt as if I had to spend my whole life making up to her for those few terrible hours.' Other mothers make light of difficulties or laugh in retrospect at events that had them in tears at the time. Therefore the family history that is consciously known and shared between a mother and her children is usually different to the unconscious template that lies buried within the child's psyche. If the discrepancy between the two is only slight, a matter of degree rather than content, then the individual grows up feeling familiar with themselves, and feeling that they are content and at one with their own personalities. If there is a very great discrepancy between a child's inner, hidden world and the mother's version of the world, that child grows up uncertain that its perceptions are right, and worried about itself and its surroundings. It intuitively knows that something is not making sense, but has no firm ground from which to explore the discrepancy.

Becoming a mother is often a time when a woman begins to understand much more of what really took place between her mother and herself, and can begin to judge just how accurate her mother's version of life has been. This enables her to make comparisons between her own external conscious ideas of mothering and the inner unconscious ideas, and to reassess the balance between the two. For many women this psychological reassessment of themselves is a crucial part of the maturing process. Carole was 29 when she had her first child, a son, and she was amazed by how quickly she sunk into a pit of despair about her inability to meet the baby's needs. Prior to the birth she had consciously believed herself to have a good relationship with her own mother and to be looking forward with confidence to becoming a mother herself. But as the days and nights of disturbed sleep and baby demands began to take their toll on her psychological defences she found herself less and less able to believe that she was credible as a mother. She would sit for hours crying to her own mother on the telephone about how inadequate she was. Then one night she had a dream in which she was falling into a deep hole in the ground. Her mother was standing at the edge of this hole watching her fall, saying 'How can I trust you to save me when you can't even save yourself?' However much she cried out to her mother, no helping hand was forthcoming. Shocked and frightened by this dream, and worried that she was about to hurt her son, Carole came looking for therapy to help her understand what was happening.

On the first evening after her assessment session with me her mother phoned her and was appalled that her daughter was 'airing her dirty linen in public'. As Carole said to me afterwards, 'it was as if I was describing her failures to you, not my own'. This was an important clue. Carole's mother had been adopted by a rather old and distant couple when she was 18 months old. She lacked any true mothering herself and therefore when Carole was born she had expectations that her daughter would in some way fill that gap and provide mothering for her. Over the years Carole had been supportive and motherly towards her mother but could not hope to live up to her mother's expectation that having a daughter would magically erase the pain of not having had a mother. Hence deeply buried in Carole's psyche was a belief that she had failed to mother her mother adequately. This was a belief, equally deeply buried, that her mother shared. Having a child of her own had brought that unconscious belief to the surface and she began to realise that her mother was unconsciously encouraging her to experience herself as inadequate as further evidence for their shared conviction. As Carole grew in understanding of herself and her perfectly adequate mothering of her child, she also began to feel that it was unreasonable of her own mother to have such expectations of her. 'She should mother me,' Carole exploded one day. Such an obvious statement and yet for her it had the impact that set straight twenty-nine years of shared mother/daughter myth.

Some of the material that resides in the unconscious does so because it is primitive, pre-verbal material that would be difficult, perhaps impossible, to express in any usual manner of communication. When you hold someone who is howling with grief, for instance, it is obvious that no words or expressions could give vent to those feelings in the same way that a pre-language sound can. Similarly with great joy, with rage, with love, or envy: all these are hard to convey in anything other than symbolic form in language. Hence they stay in the unconscious, influencing us but not being directly communicated. Some of the material, however, is actively buried, out of sight of the conscious mind, because the individual or the immediate social environment of that individual finds its expression too frightening.

We all have a range of defence mechanisms that allows us to conduct these psychological burials and they form an important part of our coping mechanisms. Given that a great majority of children and adults have to face hardships, losses, betrayals, failures, and their own eventual death, it is not surprising that we need a system of maintaining an inner equilibrium against the impact of these events. Such defences only become a problem when they are too large or too small. Defences that grow to great proportions often do so in childhood as a response to the child fearing that it will be overwhelmed by events. The only response to that fear is to increase the size of psychological defences, but these can then become 'stuck' at a high level throughout adult life. These people never deal with any distressing material at the time it occurs. It is rapidly buried in their unconscious minds by their over-active defences, out of sight, but as a permanent scar in their psyche that will affect their feelings, words and actions thereafter, however much they deny it. Generally children benefit from being exposed gradually to the real and sometimes terrible stresses of life. Those who are over-protected and never experience any need to prepare defences are as much at psychological risk as those who are exposed to events with which they cannot cope.

If there are experiences of mothering that threatened to overwhelm the child, experiences of separation for instance, then it is likely that these experiences will be buried in the unconscious mind and not readily available to thought or discussion. When people speak about their expectations of mothering they will be relating the content of their remembered experience but often their story will be coloured by the emotional memories of the other, unconscious memory of the event. I have seen a number of women who desperately wanted to have children and yet were so terrified by the thought of labour that they could not take the risk of becoming pregnant. Such women often say things like 'I know this is illogical. There is no reason for me to feel this but . . .' It is particularly important for anyone with distressing feelings that appear not to make sense consciously to understand that this is not because they are illogical, unreasonable or stupid, but rather because their buried inner world is at odds with their outer thinking world. The outer world is not always 'right'. Indeed the clues that come from our inner worlds, if we can have enough belief in ourselves to trust them, can open the windows on our personal experience, very much like letting in fresh spring air into a house long shut over the winter.

For women that fear labour there are often two interwoven threads of experience that lead them to have these basic anxieties. Firstly, there are the messages from their own mothers about the nature of birth. These messages can be covert or overt. Until fifteen or twenty years ago most fathers were 'protected' from the labour of their wives and birth of their children. This reflects social hang-ups about the female body and about the process of birth. So for the majority of mothers recently their experience of labour was occurring in different social conditions to that of their mothers. The covert message about birth of our parents' generation were being actively over-turned with a surprising speed, a speed which left some woman (and their husbands) fearful. Social change about an event as important as birth can be wonderfully liberating for those involved in the change and terrifying for those who still believe in the covert messages from their own mothers.

Secondly, a major thread that runs through our society is a religious understanding about the nature of labour. The notion that women should suffer in labour is inherent in much of our cultural understanding. Hence whenever labour is portrayed in literature it will appear to have the impact of an express train that takes a woman completely by surprise and knocks her over. This image is so unlike the labours that I have witnessed, experienced or heard described that it must be rising out of our inner needs to believe that our births knocked our mothers over and, for some at least, made them suffer.

I have also seen several women in therapy who are the adopted daughters of women who have never given birth. In this situation the daughter receives the message that her mother's mother imparted about labour and pregnancy without the intervention of the mother's own experience of the event. Such messages may be out-dated and intensified by the mother's inability or unwillingness to have children herself. One woman described this to me thus: 'My mother said that pregnancy was an envelope of fear that engulfed women.'

What becomes clear in this discussion is the extent to which the mother/daughter relationship is focal during pregnancy and early mothering. However, men also had mothers, and have feelings, usually strong ones, on the subject of mothering. In this context men have a distinct psychological disadvantage because, unlike daughters, they cannot themselves become pregnant, experience labour or experience mothering from the perspective of providing rather than consuming it. They are prone, therefore, to finding it hard to reassess the internal, mostly unconscious feelings of being mothered. During those days from conception to the first child's first birthday, most women experience a substantial shift in their understanding of their relationship with their own mother as well as their relationship with themselves as a mother. For most fathers this shift does not occur. They may come to reassess their fathers, although usually this happens at a later stage of parenting, but they are unlikely to be involved enough in the intensity of adult/baby relationships in the first six months to stimulate rethinking and re-experiencing of those early days themselves.

Given that men still have the powerful say in forming our culture, in literature, art, science, politics, economics, and in what is 'normal' for relationships, their view of mothering without the advantage of refined adult re-perceptions is the one that predominates. This is particularly true in the world of psychoanalysis where male notions of what constitutes a mature woman or a 'proper' family still hold sway. For several generations these theorists have defined what mothering is, what mothering should hope to achieve, what women should do in order to be good mothers, and, in their analysis of troubled adults, pointed the finger at the bad mother as if she were the cause of all evils. Such formulations ignore the fact that most mothers are remarkably socially powerless to challenge and change life for themselves, let alone their children. They are only allowed to make changes within the guidelines of what the culture accepts. That culture is laid down, in the most part, by men who have child memories of mothering, with all its inconsistencies and misunderstandings, and who have avoided the adult reality of parenting young children which would undoubtedly change and moderate their notions of mothers. Once, while still a medical student, I met the wife of a famous writer on child-care, a man who set a model followed by two or three generations of women as to how to be a good mother. His wife said to me with much obvious bitterness, 'If he met one of his own children in the street he probably wouldn't recognise them.' His writing, his understanding, his experience of mothering had to be of being mothered and yet his word was taken as gospel by many women who believed that from the limits of his child experience he knew more than they, who were involved in the adult version.

For those who have a lack of experience of adult provision of parenting and therefore base their theories, assumptions and instructions on their half-remembered experiences of

being mothered as a child, life as a parent can seem
straightforward; they can have a certainty about what is
'right'; they can afford to be critical of others and unques-
tioning about themselves. They may be fired by a driving
ambition to change mothering into a more loving and giving
process than they themselves received; they may believe
their own mothers to have been perfect and judge all other
women against that model of perfection; they may feel
angry towards their own mothers and therefore by connection with all mothers; they may feel envious of women who
can become mothers like the mother they would have liked
to identify with more strongly. Whatever their feelings,
without re-experiencing the event from 'the other side' they
will have no chance to firstly locate such feelings consciously, to give them acknowledgment and acceptance,
and secondly to reassess such feelings against a backcloth of
reality.

For instance, I was a therapist to a man who had felt
violently angry with his wife in the first six months of them
becoming parents. He was ashamed of these feelings and
never acted out on them. He recognised them to be 'the feelings of a monster from my depths', and wanted to understand consciously what was happening to him. We spent
many hours talking about his own mother, someone who
preoccupied his thoughts at this moment of his life. She had
been widowed when he was 4, and he had three other
brothers, all under 10 at the time. He had always tried to be
'the good boy' and not bother his mum, and yet beneath this
was consumed with rage that she had so little energy or time
for them all. When their own baby was 4 weeks old his
mother had come to visit and had had a long chat with her
daughter-in-law about how difficult she had found it looking
after four young children on her own. This had led to this
man's wife making several sympathetic comments about
his mother to him along the lines of 'now I've had a baby I
think I begin to understand just how overwhelmed your
mum must have felt'. Several days later he began to feel
violently angry with his wife, based, he thought, on a belief
that she was going to be a bad mother to his son. As therapy
progressed he made it clear to me that he thought all women

were likely to be bad mothers. When I took a fortnight's holiday he commented that such neglect was to be expected. I was after all a woman too. This led to us exploring how realistic his desires for a perfect mum were. He began to see that his wife was exhausted trying to be the perfect mum and that whatever she did was never quite enough. His constant demands and criticism of her were handicapping and not helping her and his son. He became very sad about the loss of his father, someone he had not consciously considered for many years. In many ways his fury with his mother had been a good defence against the sadness of losing a dad when he was so young. That defence helped him when he was 4 to cope with a tragedy, but had become a hindrance to his becoming an effective father, and an effective husband to the mother of his son when he was 28.

As children we experience relationships with other children as well as important adults. For many of us there were few other children within the close family while we were children and so these relationships were formed with the children of friends of our parents, our school friends, and the more distant circle of relatives. Such relationships probably lacked the intensity that marks sibling relationships. We have no need to feel envious of our friends' attachments to our parents for instance, whereas siblings often experience intense envy and rivalry for their mother's attention. Conversely we have few people of our own age who shared the experience of being parented in our home at the same time, and, for many, this represents something of a loss; no comrades in the battle with parents during adolescence.

Smaller families also mean that few young adults have experience in looking after babies. Many women face motherhood with a few nights' babysitting as their only previous experience; some do not even have that. Women who have acted as little mothers to large families have the necessary experience, but may feel bitter about that early role and unwilling to repeat it in adult life with their own children. Children who have been disrupted by the birth of a new baby in the family when they were already into their teens may also become so horrified by the reality of a baby that they say 'not for me!' The most common situation, however, is for both the new mother and father to have had no true experience of their roles, and for them to be isolated geographically or socially from those who could support with help and advice. Hence they begin by undertaking a crucial role from a position of extraordinary ignorance. Few of us would dream of taking on any other job that was as responsible or demanding without some guidance and some in-service training.

In recent generations the alternative to learning in large families, or from mum or an aunt next door, has been the professional advice poured onto parents about the physical and psychological well-being of the baby. The old way of passing knowledge and experience from generation to generation tended to mean that things did not change much. With the advent of professional advice the door to changing styles of parenting was open. Many of these professionals throught that they knew how to improve the lot of the baby and taught accordingly. Much old wisdom was thrown out in the light of new understandings. But, as we have seen, those new understandings tended to come from men who were taking a theoretical stance on mothering based on their own unconscious feelings about their own mothering, whereas the old-fashioned advice came mostly from women who had had children of their own, and who were therefore talking from the experience both of being mothered and being mother.

In our society we still give more weight to something a man tells us even when we think it may well be wrong. I often see young mothers who are desperately attempting to mother in the way that appeals to their partners, rather than in a way which reflects something individual and valuable about that woman as a mother. They will commonly tell me that they realise their husbands do not know much about it and yet they still follow their advice. Sometimes when I am lecturing about mothering I say that I am surprised women take so much notice of their husbands. This usually produces a laugh from all the women present, who know exactly what I mean about attempting to follow daft advice just because it comes from 'your' man. Even the creators of soap powder adverts know we will respond more favourably to a man telling us to use certain products even though most of us know very well that women are the undoubted 'experts' on washing! For soap powders it may not matter too much whose advice you take but when it comes to a style of mothering, the real thing, the uniqueness of that mother with that child, is always preferable for both woman and baby than some well-meant but unknowledgeable advice.

One of the major drawbacks to such advice is that it will not prepare mothers for how they will feel. Based as it is on men's ideas from the experience of being mothered rather than mothering, it is bound to be baby-orientated and fail to cover what it feels like to be a mother. There are a number of powerful emotions connected with mothering for which most mothers are totally unprepared. The two most often mentioned are anger and anxiety. Most women will admit to feeling more angry with their children, particularly when they are babies, than with anyone else in the world. This is hardly surprising given that it is those babies who will be making impossible demands, at the time when the mother is most tired and yet most wanting to do her best. Perhaps the levels of anxiety connected to mothering are more surprising. Mothers worry about the health and welfare of their babies. A common situation was summed up for me in a therapy group when a young mother said, 'I was beside myself just wanting him to go to sleep at last. I felt like I'd been awake for ever and I just did not know what to do for him. Then all of a sudden he fell asleep and then I was so worried that he might stop breathing that I had to get up every few minutes and check on him.' The anxiety can generalise beyond the baby, to the mother herself, to her close environment, when the home suddenly becomes a frightening and threatening place, or to the world at large, when the mother may avoid going out at all because she is so frightened.

It is often the fact that these emotions are unexpected that makes them so difficult to deal with. Mothers who are prepared for the personal onslaught cope with more humour and self-understanding. They tend to be less critical of themselves or their feelings, responding to them in a more matter-of-fact manner, rather than castigating themselves and believing every unexpected feeling to be a measure of their inadequacies as mothers. The more those in her close environment know and feel comfortable themselves with the real emotions of mothering, the more the woman will feel free to openly discuss these experiences and to begin to rate them as just that . . . experiences . . . part of the rich pattern of mothering. If, however, a woman is surrounded by people who have not experienced mothering themselves or have forgotten whatever they did experience, then it may be very difficult to admit to hating the baby as much as she loves it, to feeling wildly angry as well as gently caring, to feel envious of all the love and attention lavished on the baby when suddenly she feels vulnerable and in need of help herself. When such mothers do get up the courage to talk about these experiences they often get labelled as bad mothers, and families may punish them in many ways, overt and covert, for such admissions.

I hope in this book to look towards an image of the 'true' mother as opposed to the 'perfect' mother. Perfection in mothering is never more than a good all-giving façade, a façade which may well puzzle the growing child and leave it believing that all that is wrong in itself, its parents and the world is its own fault, as its mother is too perfect to be to blame. 'True' mothers learn to take the risk of being themselves with their children. They learn to do this in public as well as in private. There is no point in telling a child you love them if that is not the truth at that moment. There is no point in pretending to be angry or threatening dire punishments if you do not mean it. In every relationship it is the truth in our expressions to each other which lead to what is valuable and lasting. Having a false self, however much that self may seem like the socially acceptable good mum of the year, will not satisfy the average baby who knows a great deal about what goes on by observation of its mother. Mothers who find themselves as women and as people through the experience of mothering will find it a remarkable process, more fraught and yet more wonderful than any other relationship. Women who try to submerge themselves into other people's notions of how they should mother, whether that other person is their husband, their mother or an expert, will lose themselves and eventually their relationship with the child. Being good enough is what counts. Being honest about how limited good enough sometimes is but managing to struggle through, mother and child learning together as the relationship grows, is to pay your child the respect that she or he deserves as a new and one day independent person.

2
THE POWER OF PREGNANCY

THE DECISION TO CONCEIVE

Motherhood can be the best or worst emotional experience
of a woman's life. Usually it is a complex mixture of both
of these extremes and all that lies between them. Most girls
grow up believing that they will have children and that this
will give them credibility as women as well as providing a
fundamental form of fulfilment. The facts that it will also
make them emotionally vulnerable, place severe practical
limits around their lives, and require that they rapidly
achieve heights of adult responsibility that few other situations in life demand are often the hidden cost of the
experience.

The belief that we can make a rational decision about
whether or not we want that experience seems to me to be
a myth. Instead it is often from a position of relative
ignorance women make the decision to do something from
which there is no turning back. Having made this supposedly
free decision they are then confronted by powerful social
dictates to the effect that they are meant to carry the complete responsibility for its consequences however unpredictable these may be. An understanding of the nature of the
decision to conceive, even if this is retrospective, is often
helpful to parents who are struggling to cope with the long-
term nature of the task of parenting. So although women
may seem to make the final decision about conception there
is a complex series of influences which colour that end-point,
and the conscious desires of the woman are not by any
means always the strongest of those influences.

Most psychological theories of development view the decision to become parents as an important step towards increasing adult maturity. They place particular emphasis on the necessity of the experience of mothering for obtaining maturity in women. In common with all experiences, mothering only increases an individual's emotional maturity if the woman is willing to be self-observant, emotionally honest and open to change. Hence, simply being a mother will not in itself ensure that a woman then becomes mature. Conversely it is also possible for women to obtain adult maturity without becoming a mother. The form and extent of our maturity directly reflects our experience in life and what we make of that experience. Thus a decision not to become a mother or a woman discovering that she cannot become a mother sets that woman onto a different path towards a different understanding of self and a different set of experiences. Motherhood, because it is time-consuming and often overwhelming, prevents many women from having other adult experiences which can significantly add to an individual's maturity: extensive travel, socialising and single-mindedly following a career, for example. The experience of mothering offers a unique opportunity to review our own development psychologically in the light of an adult observation of our children's experience. Such a review can make remarkable changes to the individuals' understanding of themselves and strongly influence the pattern of their adult maturity. The total giving, emotionally and practically, that motherhood involves is also, for many women, a unique experience and one that they value in their overview of themselves as mature adults.

The fantasy of perfection

Although it is thought of as the central experience of a woman's life, the reality of mothering tends to remain something of a mystery, leaving the would-be mother with only the images of her fantasies as a guide. Such images will be far removed from the reality she discovers once her baby has arrived. At best, in these circumstances, motherhood is a surprise, at worst an enormous disappointment.

There is a lack of factual knowledge about what is involved in caring for a baby because the majority of us come from families that are too small to have exposed us to the experience as adolescents and hence we have no way of predicting what our response to this particular form of stress will be. We will also only have the verbal history of how our parents coped with such a stress to base our images on and this is likely to be a rather whitewashed version of the real thing. It is interesting how quickly most parents forget the difficult and even ugly aspects of parenting when they come to recite that experience to their growing children. We are often unaware of the images of parenting with which we have been bombarded by the media, literature, religion and a variety of other sources. These images usually stress the loving, caring and happy aspects of the experience. Mums on television adverts are not depressed or enraged. Babies exposed to our view tend to be of the washed, fed and quiet variety. These sources are therefore only imparting a partial and distorted knowledge about the experience.

A decision to conceive that is based on these partial truths and fantasies is a rocky foundation for an experience that is far from ideal for everyone. It is a particularly dangerous base for the idealistic would-be mother if she is surrounded by a husband and family who share her ideals. The reality of the experience will rapidly offer her opportunities to reassess the fantasies and, if she has the emotional space within her relationships to do so, this experience will change her in ways that enhance her coping with the reality as she finds it. If family and husband, protected from the enormity of the baby's demands themselves, continue to maintain the ideals and fantasies, then the woman can become isolated and disillusioned with herself. Nothing can be more harmful to both the mother's and baby's emotional futures than the early feelings of failure in mothers who are judging themselves and being judged by others against fantasies rather than ordinary 'good enough' mothers.

The role of society in the decision to conceive

Families need their womenfolk to have children if that family is to survive. Taking a wider view societies also have this need. In communities that have been ravaged by war or disaster birth rates often rise as if the society can compel groups of individual women to act as an organised mass and fulfil its need to replace the lost people. In situations of overcrowding or shortage of resources we are encouraged to decrease the birth rate. Most of us like to believe that the decision to have a child is a personal and rational decision and yet when looked at in this more global way it is clear that that is by no means the entire truth. The culture and the time in which you live greatly influences that decision. It does so in two ways. Firstly communities can give overt messages about fertility. They can value it or they can express anxiety about the extent of it. Secondly there are also covert messages. Some of these can be obvious in their intent even if they do not overtly spell out the attitudes behind it: there can be financial incentives to restrict or enlarge families or birth-control methods can be made easily available or illegal. However, many covert messages are subtle and difficult to recognise. We tend to swallow them without realising that we have been influenced. For instance the two-adult, two-children image of a 'normal' family is the most commonly depicted in children's books in Britain. We take in this image of normality at the same time as learning to read. Such a norm is obviously quite different to that accepted in many other cultures, for example those countries strongly influenced by Roman Catholic tradition or those where poverty is rife and children still represent a couple's only possible 'wealth' and security in old age.

These messages are often confused and even contradictory. A society, like a family or an individual, can be mixed up about what it wants. At the present time in the UK we are educating women and hoping that they will pursue careers outside of their homes, but at the same time we give those women messages about the need to be at home with their babies and have almost no organised child-care services. The society is confused about what it wants from its women, who are thus left to sort out that confusion individually. Of course, in a democracy, it is an important privilege that we are left to sort out public confusion by individual decision but this is a rather mixed blessing when the public confusion is denied or at least hidden from popular debate, and only demonstrated in covert ways.

At a deeper level I believe that British culture is confused about the value of children. Although we may pay lip service to the wonder of new life much of the way our adult lives are organised seems to actively exclude children, and therefore also exclude any adult who has to be with those children. Hence working and social situations outside of our homes are not 'user-friendly' towards children. We do not have crêches or interesting playrooms in our hospitals, our factories or our offices. We do not allow children in pubs, or welcome them in restaurants, theatres and churches. They are seen as an unwelcome distraction from the 'real' adult business in progress. Adult business and those who pursue it are without doubt given more prestige, power and economic reward than any activity dealing with children. Those parents who have taken small children on holiday or to live in other countries rapidly understand how children are more acceptable elsewhere. Young children are a common and welcome sight in French, Spanish, Italian or Greek restaurants. Life in many African countries revolves around adult involvement in child-care. In most non-Western societies children are regarded as a blessing not just at birth but throughout their childhood.

Women in Britain are left to deal individually with a major social conflict throughout their lives. On the one hand they are fed, from infancy, with the notion that an important part of their role is to be a mother, that this is a worthwhile and valuable exercise to their community as well as to themselves. They are led to believe that they will be praised and supported for this activity, that their fertility will be welcomed. There is an obvious truth about these overt messages. Of course all societies need their women to be available to the idea of having children. On the other

hand society delivers a second set of messages, a more subtle and covert set which often go unnoticed by women until
they are mothers. Amongst these messages lie the uncomfortable notions that the society does not like children and
that, far from appreciating the efforts of women to provide
the next generation, it actively seeks to punish them for this
activity by excluding them from the 'real' adult business of
life, and failing to reward them financially or in any other
way.

Seeing conception as an entirely personal decision may be
one of the ways that many women have used to avoid the
pain involved in facing this social contradiction. We want to
believe that we can hold ourselves above the confusion of
the mass and make a decision that is based solely in our own
needs. Undoubtedly more available and reliable contraception combined with the legalisation of abortion has given
women more scope for choice. However, it is a choice made
within the boundaries of the woman, her family, and her
community. It is a decision which is bound to be heavily influenced by her surroundings. If a woman insists on taking
all the responsibility for that decision, then she also tends
to carry all the disillusionment and guilt. If she has some
understanding of the context within which she makes the
decision she has more chance of allotting responsibility
more evenly among other family members and the community as a whole.

Not understanding the social context of mothering can be
a major source of discontent in new mothers. I have seen
many women who suffer overwhelming disappointment
because of their partner's and families' lack of positive
response to their pregnancies. They comfort themselves
with the feeling that all this will change once the baby
arrives. But then they discover that after the first few days
the world does not open its arms to them, but rather slams
doors in their faces. Any notion that they are precious individuals now that they are mothers is rapidly eradicated by
a visit to a post-natal clinic where they wait for hours in
order to spend a few minutes with a doctor who may be a
stranger. He (and even now nine times out of ten it is still
a he) will want to reassure them that they are physically

well but is unlikely to be interested in their emotional experience of mothering so far. Many women leave their post-natal examinations feeling like machines that have just been given the go-ahead to get back into production. Rather than it being an experience of affirmation for the new mother as a person it becomes another moment of feeling abandoned and ignored.

I have heard many mothers comment that they felt they had suddenly become faceless non-adults once they had a child. They complain that people talk to them and treat them differently. This is particularly painful because they imagined that once they were mothers they would enter the world of grown-up women, thereby gaining acknowledgment and respect for their womanliness. Instead they often feel like social outcasts, who are thrown into a twilight world with no way of knowing how long their alienation will last.

I think the women who survive the traumas of disillusionment with the social experience of mothering best are those who have close, non-critical relationships with other women. It may be that these women have more accurate notions of what motherhood involves from the beginning, but also such friendships seem to protect women from the social confusions by affirming the woman as a person in the eyes of other adults. The experience of being 'seen' as what and who you are somewhere makes the experience of being invisible elsewhere more bearable. The women who survive least well seem to be those who are already alienated from a personal source of affirmation prior to the birth. Those women who have poor relationships with their own mothers, who have young or immature husbands, who work in totally male environments, or who have not had an opportunity to make non-work friends prior to the birth are all more at risk of being hurt by the responses of the outside world because they will not receive enough positive messages about themselves to outweigh the negative ones they will receive from a confused society.

Undoubtedly the social context of any woman influences her decision to both conceive and to continue the pregnancy and is in that way powerful in determining the pattern of her

life. However, societies are not good at accepting responsibilities for the children whose births they have influenced,
rather wishing to see that responsibility as resting entirely
with the parents, and, in reality, usually with the mother.
Hence society feels free to spell out what it thinks is 'good
mothering' and to judge and condemn women who fall short
of those criteria without feeling any obligation to provide
practical support, encouragement or reward for the job. This
split between the power to influence and the acceptance of
responsibility for the consequences causes much bitterness
and resentment in women, who feel quite literally left
'holding the baby' on behalf of everyone else.

The role of the family in the decision to conceive

As any family therapist will tell you, families are powerful
systems which place pressures on the individual members
in order to maintain some form of equilibrium within the
family unit as a whole. Within healthy families these
pressures are exerted fairly. By negotiation and compromise
the needs of each member are met and demands between
members are aportioned evenly. But in many families the
burden of caring for both young and old falls on one
member. This member often services the needs of all the
other family members at the same time as fulfilling the
responsibilities of the family as a whole towards its
vulnerable and needy members. Conventionally this
member is the mother-figure.

We have become used to the family system over many
generations of evolution and are led to believe that it is a
system specifically developed to help protect women and
children. This supposed protection has always had a cost
however. Until this century men owned their wives and
children as much as any other form of property. Today, at
weddings, we play at the father 'giving away' his daughter
but only four generations ago that play was for real and
encapsulated in a single moment the central transaction of
society whereby daughters were passed from one family to
another. Women were used as tokens of communication
between families at many levels of society. This human

matrix bonded families into larger and larger groups, holding societies together by interrelationships. Such a function for women is very obvious in the choosing of wives for kings, thereby bonding nations together, but was equally important at every level of social functioning as a means of bonding families together.

Having been given to a strange family the women were then the property of their husbands. Any children they produced were also the property of that man. It is hard to see why we should imagine that such a system was designed to be of benefit to women and children. Indeed we know that then as now many women and children were abused by their menfolk but had no power or rights to correct the situation. Indeed it seems much more likely to many writers on this issue (e.g., Juliet Mitchell) that the system of families were designed to allow men certainty about the paternity of their male offspring who would eventually inherit from them. The suggestion that families as a system evolved for the good of men seems to be increasingly reflected in research that details men's and women's experience of marriage today. Twice as many women as men will say they are unhappy with their relationships and it is women who make up the majority of those seeking divorce.

Of course times have changed and the law now makes it very clear that men cannot consider they have proprietal rights over their families. Despite that, I am faced many times each year with family situations of violence, neglect, irresponsibility and incest, in which it seems as if that concept of male ownership is still a strongly held belief. It is a belief that remains embedded within a police system reluctant to interrupt domestic violence, within a psychiatric system that is sometimes guilty of judging a woman's mental health on her ability to meet her husband's needs, and within much of the doctrine of family normality handed out day in and day out by the media. It is as if the law has gone ahead in its changing view of ownership within families but that many people are emotionally lagging behind in that change. Even among those who speak of freedom and equal rights within families, and who believe in these concepts with their conscious minds, are many who would openly admit to not reaching such ideals in reality.

We are all touched by the roots of our experiences. The relationships of our parents, grandparents and great-grandparents haunt us in memories that influence us powerfully even when we are hardly aware of them. So when a woman comes to decide about conceiving a child, she is usually making that decision within the context of a relationship with a man and his family. It remains most usual for a woman to make this decision within the context of a marriage to that man or within the context of wishing to be married to the man. She may make the decision to conceive with or without his knowledge or agreement. Such a decision is within her power, but as soon as she has conceived she becomes part of a complex system within the child's father's family. The child will usually bear their name, a different name to the mother's original name, and so symbolically at least can be seen as belonging to the man's family and not her own.

Hence embodied in the conception is a powerful transaction between the woman and the man and his family. She may well have the power to conceive or not, in her own time. She can horrify the parents of the young men 'trapped' into marriage by their girlfriends' pregnancies or she can delight the mother-in-law anxious to be a granny. She can fulfil her husband's desire to be a father or present him with a pregnancy at an impossible time. She can conceive to fit her own internal needs or as a response to all those around her. However, from the second of conception the balance of power begins to change. The baby is increasingly a family member and not simply her decision. Women who choose to conceive children without marrying, living with, or even naming the father, may be looking for a solution to the problems that this powerful transaction causes many women.

In modern families this transaction can lead to many misunderstandings between generations. We have changed our patterns of family life. Young families are often geographically separated from their parents and, as there is increasing intensity of commitment between partners in marriages, so there is an equal and opposite slackening of their commitment to their families of origins. The grannies who feel they have the right to have a say in the child's upbringing and who would have been a powerful influence four generations ago now may face the cold shoulder to their advice. Many couples choose to deliberately distance their relatives in order to minimise their 'interference' in the moulding of the new family. Resistance to marriage is partly at least a way of holding the power of both families at bay in the lives of the individuals concerned. The fact that so many couples eventually go on to marry is not a sign of their weakness of commitment to non-marital relationships but rather a sign of the massive strength that families and society have to make individuals conform at some point.

It is rapidly apparent at times of crisis however that the old models of family life are never far beneath the surface. When a child is born with a handicap, grandparents as much as parents will feel threatened and anxious. If a child is ill the parent will often intuitively turn to one of their own parents for support and advice, and may feel very bitter if this is not forthcoming. Even in the day-to-day stresses of early parenting, the sleepless nights and the sense of frustration engendered by a small crying baby, each parent will turn back to the notions of family life they learnt within their families of origin. If they came from similar families this may bring them together as they cope with the stresses. If their families of origin coped with problems in very different ways, this turning back to past experience will cause a rift between them. So even in new and modern families separated from their parents and grandparents, actively wanting to produce a different form of family life and within a social context which no longer gives legal credence to the man's ownership, there is a tendency to resort to what was familiar when under stress.

Undoubtedly women's lives have changed in just one generation. Over the last four or five generations they have changed greatly. One of the greatest changes is in the pattern of marital or co-habiting relationships with its new impetus for equality. Women may make the decision to conceive within a relationship that they see as very different to their parents' and their partners' parents' relationships. However, becoming parents may well be the stimulus that takes them back to a much older pattern of relating, and that pattern will almost certainly offer the woman less equality and more responsibility for assuming the burden of caring within the family. Of course many women do not know this and are therefore shocked, humiliated and disillusioned to discover patterns of behaviour in their partners, their families and themselves that they thought they had eradicated to their own advantage in this generation.

The woman's family is not without a major role in influencing the decision to conceive. A daughter's relationship with her mother may be so close that it is they rather than women and partner who decide when it would be right to have a baby. Such mothers often live close by and will play a major part in the rearing of the child. Indeed the arrival of grandchildren may make these mothers' lives feel worthwhile again. Hence they will place pressures on the daughters to conceive as quickly as possible. In the meantime the man may feel very differently about the situation, wanting time alone with his partner and a chance to further their education or income. The daughter/wife then becomes torn between the two or makes a decision that favours one or the other. Any decision in this situation carries important consequences for the future. A distancing in close mother/daughter relationships may leave the daughter feeling lonely and depressed, but a choice to agree with mother carries with it the threat of an unwilling father and an aggrieved partner. In such situations there is an element of no-win for the woman involved. Another situation in which a mother/daughter relationship influences this decision is becoming increasingly common as women become more educated and enter professions or business careers. Women who become more successful than their mothers in the external world often feel increasingly emotionally distant from their mothers. It becomes difficult to talk to them or share intimate experiences when the daughter's experiences are very different to those of her mother. The mother may be very proud of her daughter and be encouraging her to continue her success, but many daughters in this situation long to be able to identify with mother once again and return to their old closeness. One of the ways in which a daughter may feel she can achieve that closeness is to become a mother herself.

This decision can have unexpected consequences for the woman involved. Firstly the closeness they seek with their mothers is often an illusion. For some reason they have never really been close and the mother is comfortable with that whilst the daughter yearns for the closeness of her fantasies. Secondly the mother may be heavily invested in her daughter's success and worried that pregnancy will prevent further advance in that direction. Thus this daughter will find, once pregnant, that far from being closer to her mother, she may well be pushed away in anger.

Finally mothers react to their daughters' decisions about pregnancy in the context of their own experience and their own needs. Mothers who enjoyed mothering and had the children they wished to have, happily and safely, may be easily delighted that their daughters too will have children. But many mothers have difficult and traumatic memories of attempting to conceive, having miscarriages, stillbirths, losing babies and other children, experiencing difficulties with mothering or not being able to have as many children as they wanted because of social or relationship pressures. For these mothers the thought that their daughters may become pregnant is tainted with envy, jealousy, anxiety, and a reawakening of their own past sadness. Such mothers give their daughters messages about their feelings both verbally and non-verbally and may be very influential in a daughter's decision because of the intensity of their own feelings.

A woman's role in the decision to conceive

We have seen that a woman making this decision is involved in a complex matrix of relationships which will each make its own contribution to her decision. These contributions may well be at odds with each other. It is the woman who is the endpoint of the decision making. It is an awesome responsibility which many dodge by simply 'forgetting' to take a pill or 'taking a chance'. In this way they can leave fate in the laps of the gods. Only three or four generations ago most women had little choice but to bow to fate. Now some at least choose to take the decision into their own hands.

In order to make a decision a woman has to balance internal and external values and practicalities. At some stage in their lives a number of women describe a sense of compulsion to have a child. Once experienced it tends to propel them into pregnancy whatever the social, educational or career consequences are. Quite where such an intense internal compulsion arises is a matter of debate. Some would say it is nature's way of pushing healthy young women into pregnancies when they are most physically and mentally ready. There may well be some basic truth in this notion but it is probably only a partial truth. The compulsion is as likely to arise from some social or relationship issue outside of the woman as from her own intuitive sense of readiness. Hence many women still choose to conceive in an attempt to mend broken relationships or bond their men to them. Other women conceive as a solution to their sense of loneliness in life. Many women, especially those with low self-esteem, experience pregnancy as the only time that they contain something worthwhile. Thus whenever they feel unloved or threatened with alienation from important others they may feel a compulsion to become pregnant.

Certainly I have known many women over the years who 'replace' the children that are taken into care, adopted, fostered or aborted with new pregnancies embarked upon rapidly after the loss of the other child. Indeed, until quite recently it was recommended that mothers who had had stillbirths went ahead and had another baby as quickly as possible to alleviate their sadness. Nowadays that advice seems callous. Most of us know that one child can never replace another and that women who lose children need time to grieve that loss before embarking on further pregnancies. Even with the advice to take time after one loss before the next conception many women still go ahead because being pregnant again deadens the sense of pain and grieving. Sadly it only has this effect until after the delivery of the child and then the mother is faced with a return of her unresolved grief for the dead child together with the demands of the new living child, who can never be as perfect as the dead one is in the mother's fantasies.

Reading through this you may wonder what are the 'normal' reasons for deciding to conceive and how does any woman ever know what decision to make and for what reasons she is making that decision. In the final analysis the decision is often made with a mixture of conscious and unconscious awareness. Although we now have the power of knowledge to prevent conception we do not have as much power to guarantee conception when and where we want it. Thus a decision not to conceive is more easily put into practice than a positive decision for conception. Some women fear that they cannot wait any longer before making the decision and therefore take the leap with a 'now or never' attitude whilst others become pregnant just as soon as they can to see whether they can.

In different circumstances and as members of different families we would all make different decisions. Each decision is neither right nor wrong but merely the end product of many competing and contradictory forces. Women are powerful as never before in the making of that decision and yet still that power looks quite laughable when compared to the thrust of all the other influences on the final moment when conception occurs, a new life begins, and the mother's life changes for ever.

The experience of pregnancy

Once pregnant many women experience ambivalent feelings about their situation. However much the pregnancy was wanted, once achieved it will stir up anxieties as well as delights. During pregnancy anxieties centre around the health of the foetus and once born around the forming of the child's personality. Much pressure is placed on women to be responsible for both the health and personality of the baby from the early days of pregnancy. They are encouraged to give up smoking and alcohol, take iron supplements and rest, do exercises and behave generally in ways that protect the foetus. If they fail to do this society tends to condemn them. They are also 'educated' during this time about labour and motherhood beyond. Expectations about mothering are fed to them along with the vitamin pills.

Society assumes that from the moment of conception a mother will unambivalently want to do, think and feel only those things that are to the child's advantage. How wonderful it might be if all women could be such saints! However, they are but human despite being pregnant. Indeed they are not only human but also in a period of change and stress. Most of us need to feel that there is some flexibility in our lives and that we have control and power over our environment. This is particularly true at times of change and stress. A sense of being out of control is anxiety-provoking and this is most true if we feel that our internal world is out of control as well as our external world.

Pregnancy is often experienced as an invasion of the woman's inner world and I have heard women talking bitterly about their 'little cancer' within as a way of expressing their horror about feeling out of control. The body changes and may become unfamiliar to the woman. Pregnancy is a clear label both that the person is a woman and that she is sexually active. Many women like to emotionally deny their femaleness, dieting themselves into more masculine shapes and dressing asexually. There are many reasons for women to feel and behave like this and pregnancy is often the only time in their lives when they feel exposed as women and therefore vulnerable and even despicable. I have heard more fiercely expressed contempt for their own bodies amongst pregnant women than in any other situation. For women who did not like their bodies prior to pregnancy, it provides further fuel for their dissatisfaction. Of course, at the other end of the spectrum there are some women who feel and look more happy with their bodies when pregnant than at any other time. They seem to positively glow and appear to maintain their sense of internal control despite rapid changes. For them pregnancy is a confirmation of their internal value as women and is therefore not experienced as an emotional or physical threat.

Pregnancy also clearly marks the woman as sexually active and again this is a label with which many women feel uncomfortable. A woman's sexuality is an area of great social and personal confusion. Society is unclear about whether women are meant to be sexy, and if so, at whom is that sexiness meant to be directed. Hence women are left to make sense of messages that tell them their breasts are sexual stimuli if exposed on page three, the normal way of feeding babies if attached to a new mother and a potential source of sexual satisfaction to themselves if they belong to the groups of women who can acceptably seek sexual gratification. Pregnant women are caught in the middle of that confusion because, while it is clear they must have been recently sexually active in order to be pregnant, mothers and mothers-to-be are not assumed to be sexual. Hence there is a puzzling change in their assumed sexuality best described as a switch from seducing to producing. These assumptions are not based on the feelings of individual women but rather some general overview of the sexuality of a whole sex as seen by the opposite sex. I am always amazed at just how many men truly believe that their own mothers were not sexual. I have long suspected that the entire concept of immaculate conception represents the male need to see his mother as an untouched virgin.

However, many women feel just as sexy when pregnant as at any other time. Certainly mothers can be sexual. These experiences of sexuality may be unexpected and worrying for women who believed the assumptions of the male society which surrounds them. It may be particularly worrying if the husband also believes the assumptions about mothers being non-sexual. It is not unusual for such men to have affairs while their wives are pregnant as a way of avoiding a realisation that pregnant women can be sexual. Hence the woman is left with the confusion of her own sexual needs, which are unexpected and unmet, and the pain of being betrayed at a time when she needs total commitment.

As well as the confusion and false assumptions about her sexuality which may pervade her most intimate relationship there will also be a changing of style in her relationships with most of the other men she mixes with, both professionally and socially, once her pregnancy is obvious. That change will reflect the men's previous experiences of pregnant women. Those men who have delighted in their own women's pregnancies, for instance, may become solicitous and kindly, adopting a rather paternal stance to someone who only yesterday was just another colleague. Many men do not have such positive experiences however. For the man whose mother had a number of further pregnancies after his own birth pregnancy may be associated with a distancing from mother and a sense of pain and loss for himself. Other people's pregnancies may stir up painful feelings of depression and fury. For the men who envy women's abilities to bear children, pregnancy in a colleague may be like a red rag to a bull. Uterus envy is a poorly documented concept, usually denied by men, and yet when you see the destructive anger stirred up in some men by the power of pregnancy it seems obvious that such envy does exist. There is also the problem faced by small boys when they realise that they are different from their mothers and will therefore never be able to identify with and internalise their mothers in the same way that daughters can. This sense of being biologically excluded from the female world of their mothers and sisters can be painful for growing boys unless they have an equally attractive option to join the male world as represented by their relationships with their fathers. For a man who has experienced this exclusion from the female world as a trauma there may be a special need to be friendly with his female friends and colleagues as a reassurance that he is still acceptable. The discovery that one of these women is pregnant, an experience he can never have, is likely to underline for him the original sense of exclusion with all its accompanying pain and make him unreasonable and even hateful towards a woman who had previously been his friend and confidante.

For the man who likes to flirt with his secretary, her pregnancy may well be unnerving. I have heard bosses comment that pregnant secretaries lower the status of their offices. As the relationships between men and women are often defined by the degree of sexuality between them, pregnancy, with all its contradictory connections with sexuality, changes the rules of these relationships and can cause confusion and chaos for both sides.

Many women feel burdened not only by their own confusion but also by a sense of guilt for having confused the men around them. It is as if they experience themselves as responsible for their menfolk's emotional well-being and are therefore caught between conceiving the baby they both

wanted but producing a situation neither can easily understand or cope with. Anxiety and guilt are the two most commonly described feelings by women in this form of conflict.
The relationship between themselves and their men may
become distant and cold and they usually feel powerless to
influence that although also guilty about it. They may feel
that the pregnancy was a mistake and even begin to have
strongly negative feelings about the growing foetus. For
most women there are moments of anxiety about the baby's
health and normality as the months of pregnancy stretch on.
It is unusual for women not to be aware of the real dangers
of abnormality. Even uneducated women will have
neighbours or relatives who know someone with a Down's
Syndrome baby, for instance, and will wonder whether
it might happen to them too. The more educated and
informed, the more anxious mothers are likely to be.
Although statistically the numbers of deformed and sick
children, stillbirths and maternal mortalities are low, knowing that they exist at all is bound to be anxiety-provoking. For
mothers who have confused attitudes towards their babies,
and who may at times wish them dead, these anxieties grow
as they are fed by the guilt which almost always accompanies
our more hateful feelings. At one moment they may be
wishing the baby into non-existence and at the next they will
feel crippled by anxiety that something terrible may happen
to themselves or the baby as punishment for such thoughts.
This may be particularly true for mothers who have considered or even attempted abortion.

Women need to feel loved and supported, nurtured and
cared for themselves in order to withstand the demands of
motherhood. They are not bottomless sources of caring for
others with no need of replenishment for themselves,
whatever the myths may have us believe. These needs can
be easily ignored especially if the woman finds it difficult to
allow people to help her. Many women have a sense of competition with their own mothers. They determine that they
will be better and more caring with their children. For the
women who have lost their mothers, through adoption,
divorce or death, prior to becoming mothers themselves,
they may sense a vacuum in their caring environment, a

hole where the mother should be. Although many partners cope with and even enjoy this increased need for love and support from women, many more find it difficult to understand. Some will not even realise women have these needs. Those men with particularly self-denying mothers, for instance, may assume that their womenfolk have less needs once they achieve motherhood. Certainly, I have seen many women who are disillusioned with their partners' responses to their increased needs. It may be the first time in the relationship that the needs of the woman have been larger and more urgent than the needs of the man. Some couples cannot or will not make a readjustment to the changing psychological pressures. The man may fiercely reject a suggestion that he is less than adequately caring by making the woman feel that she is too demanding. A woman may choose to protect the man from the intensity of her own needs because she too is frightened by them. So, for a while at least, she denies them and may become paradoxically stronger and more capable to hide the fear inside. Probably the greatest strength in any relationship is a flexibility of response to the changing emotional needs of each other, but sadly most of us are too young when first parents to be mature enough to benefit from such a strength. Couples who have been together longer and are more mature have a great advantage here over young couples who conceive very rapidly.

Pregnancy goes on for a surprisingly long time. Many women become bored with the process and this is especially true for those who are physically uncomfortable and those who hold their lives in limbo awaiting the birth and do not get on with the business of living in the meantime. Often first pregnancies seem much longer than subsequent ones and many women lull themselves into a half-belief that nothing is really going to happen. They may need to reassure themselves that their lives are not going to change. Perhaps they are too frightened of the enormity of the change to face it until it becomes inevitable or maybe they simply do not realise how large the changes are going to be whether they chose them or not. For these women pregnancy is a suspended state, not connected to what has gone

before or what comes afterwards. Other women cope with
the knowledge of change by making extensive practical
arrangements and buying all the 'equipment'. Feeling
prepared in this way eases the anxieties about the disrup-
tions around the corner. I feel it is important for women to
be free to prepare themselves in whatever way suits their
personalities. There is no right way of surviving the months
of confusion, change, and anxiety. Luckily, alongside those
more negative feelings sit the contentment, the eager
anticipation and the happy dreams. Pregnancy is a preparation for the strong mixture of good and bad feelings that
make motherhood such a strangely difficult and yet potentially rewarding journey. Each woman has to find her own
way towards an acceptance of those split feelings, and with
it an acceptance of herself as a good enough mother and her
baby as a good enough baby.

Pregnancy is a time for coming to know the internal world
of oneself as well as dealing with the external practicalities,
of learning to balance the importance of the two in any
future plans. I think it is a good time for women to begin to
work with the notion of being less than perfect mothers in
readiness for the future. I am convinced that the best
mothers are women who accept themselves warts and all.
Each of us can only give as mothers that which we have
been given emotionally ourselves at some time. Our
emotional bank will go into an overdraft if we try to give
that which we have not had. At some point that emotional
overdraft will be recalled and it is therefore a psychologically vulnerable state for any human being. Despite this
every generation of parents does want to give its children
something they have not had themselves. We all want an
evolution through better parenting to better people.
However good such a thought may be it places a great
burden on the people involved, children as well as parents.
Hence the need to learn to give only what you are able to
give without endangering your own internal balance. For
the vast majority of parents that will be enough for their
babies to grow and be reasonably happy. It also means that
these babies will have models of adults who know and
accept their own limits, faults and inadequacies, which will

make it a great deal easier for the baby to do the same with itself in the years ahead. This acceptance of imperfection and a recognition of all that lies within us, good and bad, is the great psychological gain of parenting. Pregnancy is the time to start the long journey towards the goal.

3

A LABOUR OF LOVE?

Most women enter labour with some apprehension. It is a time of knowing that you are alone to cope with your experience of childbirth. Only you can give birth to your child; the pleasure, pain and peril all belong to you exclusively. Despite that it is also a time of being surrounded by others who wish to help and be part of the process while not experiencing it in the personal way that you will. The sense of being alone while surrounded by others is strange and confusing to many women. The role that various helpers can be expected to play is rarely spelt out clearly. Many of those helpers will be strangers to the woman and will only know her during this stressful event in her life. Their judgments of her will therefore be based on her reaction under duress, and not her 'usual' public self. Most women drop much of their social façade during childbirth, and, unless the helpers realise they are dealing with a woman who may well be behaving quite differently from her normal self, it is all too easy for them to become involved in rapid value-judgments which are then unhelpfully transmitted back to the woman in criticisms.

Most women have expectations of some sort about the experience of labour. Sometimes these expectations come directly down to them from their mothers, aunts, sisters and close friends. Sometimes they come from the view of labour in books or on TV. Sometimes ante-natal classes with their descriptions, exercises and films make the biggest impression. Each woman has some idea of what might happen, what she would ideally like to happen and what might go wrong. These expectations are very different for different women. There are, at one end of the spectrum, those mothers who not only think they will suffer greatly during childbirth but that there is some value and 'rightness' in that suffering. They will store up their experience of suffering for many years to came, reciting it to anyone who will listen and blaming all physical problems on that experience. Although this is less common nowadays, I am still surprised at the number of women who do believe that there is a positive benefit behind experiencing pain beyond that which they would normally tolerate. Such an attitude makes labour into some sort of trial by ordeal. Sadly, some of the people sharing this view work in our obstetric departments and treat the women under their care as wimps if they dare to suggest they have a right to pain relief.

At the other end of the spectrum are those women who believe that labour is always a natural, normal and happy process producing sensations nearer to orgasm than to pain. Such a viewpoint allows them to be delightfully free from anxiety prior to delivery but does mean that some labours come as a shock or a disappointment to them. Some women expect the experience to mean very little to them, others feel it has an almost spiritual quality. To some extent expectations colour reality. Women who expect a bad time often report that they have experienced more pain and anxiety than even they predicted, while women who feel more relaxed and confident of themselves tend to feel more positive even after complicated deliveries. However, labour is a very unpredictable experience, lasting an unpredictable length of time and producing unpredictable results for both mother and child. Therefore whatever expectations a woman has, reality is likely to be rather different. For women who have several children, they discover that each labour has a reality of its own that is different to the last and therefore as unpredictable as the first.

It is this unpredictability which causes many of the problems in labour and the confusions and heated disagreements about how and where labour is best experienced. Undoubtedly women need to be able to feel secure and as relaxed as is possible. Achieving that in an obstetric department amongst machinery that resembles a torture chamber and a cast of strangers is impossible. All human beings cope better with stress and pain if they have some understanding of what is happening and some sense of remaining in control. Labour is often experienced by a woman as an inner loss of control over her own body and therefore intrinsically distressing, with or without associated pain. If the woman also feels that she has no control over her immediate environment and no idea what is going to happen next the fear associated with loss of control becomes even greater.

Given that labour is unpredictable and that most women require and want help, assistance and advice throughout the experience, there is also a need for the woman to be able to trust her helpers enough to invest some of the sense of control in them so that she can then feel more secure in relinquishing some control herself. such a psychological negotiation requires time, warmth, trust and familiarity – all the things that are in short supply in a busy delivery suite. Hence the situation often arises that the helpers take control because they feel that is the right thing to do, without going through any 'getting to know phase' with the woman involved, and therefore without her overt or covert agreement. Control is not negotiated then but simply taken from the woman, leaving her feeling defenceless in what she then perceives as hostile territory. No labour is going to be a happy affair in such circumstances. Any human being would feel frightened, pained and resentful during and after such an episode very much as if they had been attacked. Often the baby as well as the helpers is seen as an attacker and the woman feels the attack to come as much from the inside as the outside, leading to many problems for her in coping with her relationship with that child henceforth.

Home delivery offers the woman a psychologically safe and familiar place for labour. The carers are usually known and trusted and there is not any imposing or frightening machinery. Many women want to have their babies within their family circle, reassured by the presence of people and things which are everyday and normal. Despite these strong psychologically positive attributes for home deliveries it still remains unpopular with most professional carers. It is said to be difficult and costly to provide a woman with the required support for her labour in her own home. The unpredictability of labour is also often underlined to women contemplating a home delivery, with the suggestion that such a choice may place herself or the child at physical risk. For healthy women within reach of a hospital unit should difficulties arise, especially those having second or third children after uneventful, well-checked pregnancies, the risks are low for both mother and baby, and many women would choose the option of home delivery if it were more easily available. In making this choice women need to have all the information available about the rate of difficulties and their consequences for mother and baby, in a non-alarmist and helpful way, so that if the unplanned and unexpected does happen and they need rapid admission during labour they retain a feeling of knowing what is going on. For all women to have this choice there would need to be a dramatic re-arranging of our present maternity services, and much of the anxieties engendered by the subject of home deliveries is caused by fear of that massive upheaval. A small number of mothers and babies would be at high risk physically if delivered at home. The vast majority of those at risk are predictable if the pregnancy is well monitored. The group which cause most alarm to all concerned are those who develop serious and totally unexpected problems late in labour. Although this group is small numerically the fear that the lives of a healthy mother and baby may be lost is large enough to overwhelm any statistics and mean that our services tend to work against a background of knowing the worst that can happen rather than that which is much more common.

Psychological wholeness requires that we each maintain a boundary around our sense of self which marks the line between ourselves, our memories, experiences, and beliefs, and those of others, who also need personal boundaries to differentiate themselves from us. Although this boundary is a psychological entity that we cannot see or measure it is challenged when physically intrusive events happen. Hence people who are involved in accidents, for instance, and suffer physical trauma will also experience a sense of psychological insecurity connected to this challenge to their inner boundaries. If the boundary is breached or lost altogether the psyche is left defenceless from everyone and everything around. In such situations none of us could maintain 'normal' behaviour for long. For women in labour there are two dangers to her sense of 'safe-within-self boundaries'. Firstly there is a relaxing of her psychological boundaries as pregnancy advances and she begins to relate to the growing baby within. Her body is already 'invaded' by another. In real terms her boundaries have been breached. For many women this is a wonderful feeling of fullness and psychological certainty. I have heard many women say things like 'pregnancy is the time I feel most worthwhile', which is not only a reflection of social valuing of women, but often also a deeply personal sense of fulfilment. For others, however, the sense of invasion during pregnancy is disturbing. Their need to maintain complete uninterrupted boundaries cannot be met in pregnancy and they begin to feel panicky, wanting to keep everything as stable and safe in their environment as possible. If your personal boundaries are endangered, then other boundaries become desperately important: the walls of your house, the inside of your car, the close company of a few known and trusted people can all suddenly seem much more important than ever before.

In labour those personal boundaries, already psychologically breached by the pregnancy, are breached again physically. Alongside that very real sense of physical invasion or explosion come further feelings associated with loss of control, control being in the hands of strangers, the closeness of unpredictability, 'fate', all mixed with pain, stress and fear. Such experiences make further erosions into the psychological boundaries. For women who enter pregnancy with a personal sureness, a knowing of self and an acceptance of the good and bad within self, this is a challenge which can make for creative growth within the woman. From a previous position of confidence she can explore the meanings of this new challenge, learning more about herself than ever before, finding new limits to which she can go and integrating much new information in a way that leads to a leap in the maturing process. This is a healthy way for women to equip themselves for much greater challenges of motherhood in the coming weeks and months.

Sadly, many women, especially, those who are young and inexperienced and have had little opportunity to get to know self prior to pregnancy, are unprepared for this challenge. They have not had a chance to establish any sense of their own boundaries before events challenge and attack their psyches. One such woman said to me, 'I am a besieged city with nothing to protect myself.'

A mother's sense of boundaries during labour, the extent to which she can relax and feel realistically optimistic about the outcome, the negotiation to share control of self with others, the ability to survive stress, both physical and psychological, and her flexibility to allow her boundaries to change, relax then strengthen many times during the hours of labour prepare her psychologically just as the rhythmic contractions are physically preparing her. All these things will have a lasting effect on the mother/baby relationship. Mothers who experience labour as within their expectations will be psychologically stronger at the end of it and especially ready to greet the new baby with that overwhelming love and enthusiasm which can be the end-point of all the hard work. Mothers who have felt overwhelmed by their own experience, or who feel lost, abandoned, lonely, betrayed and hopeless are in no shape psychologically to embark then on important beginnings in their new relationship. One mother, after a particularly exhausting delivery which she found humiliating as well as overpowering, said to me, 'I feel as if the baby has been born through one wound and into another. My body was wounded to let him out, but something spiritual inside of me was also wounded so that where he should have met love he met anger. I think I might hate him. That wound will take a lot longer to heal than my body.'

Over the centuries the time-honoured companions of women in labour were other women, relatives and friends who had themselves had similar experiences. For the last fifteen years fathers have been encouraged to take their place in the delivery room as those who can be closest to the women without having to worry about the intricacies of the delivery itself. The helpfulness of this change to women is variable indeed. For couples who are close and understand each other the man may well be one adult that the woman wants most at her side. However, the relationship between expectant parents is not always so warm, caring and knowing of each other. Both sides can have heavily invested interests in the process which are at odds with each other. One or other may be trying to prove something about themselves or their partner. In these circumstances the closeness of the relationship becomes detrimental to the mother, adding to her burden in a situation that she may not be able to control.

One of the most common complaints women make about their labours if partners are present is that they felt that they had to protect them from much of their own anxiety or distress. This seems to be especially true if the mother thinks that something is going wrong. If alone she might well alert attention to her fears while the presence of her partner and her fear that he will react badly to her anxieties may overcome her fears for the baby. Many women do not like their partners to think they are suffering. One told me how she had refused pain relief for several hours until her husband went to get some lunch because he had often told her in the past that he could not bear to see her ill or in pain. 'I know that he gets frightened unless he believes I can cope easily,' she said, 'and so I waited until he went off for a while and then I yelled at the midwife to do something quickly to help the pain before he came back. He still tells our friends that I had no pain relief and that I floated through the whole thing effortlessly. That makes him proud. I don't think he could cope with too much of my reality.' Many women, however, find that in similar circumstances their partners can be the champions who stand up for their rights against less than helpful staff.

Another complaint women report is that staff are more likely to relate to the 'healthy' father, who is fully dressed and on his feet rather than themselves, who are in hospital nighties and lying down. This sometimes extends to the baby being handed to the father first, particularly common if the woman had a Caesarean section under epidural. It is easy to see that staff may well find it easier to relate to fathers in these circumstances but, not unreasonably, such actions make the mothers very angry. 'I felt that she wasn't my baby,' one mother said. 'I'd done all the work and they gave her to him first. They just ignored me lying there.'

Physically and psychologically, lying down in labour has serious drawbacks. Physically, mothers often experience less pain and nausea when they are upright, standing or sitting during early labour and then squatting during delivery. Labour may proceed more rapidly when the mother is in an upright position than when she is horizontal. Psychologically women usually feel more 'themselves' if they are allowed to stand, sit or walk. Many of us associate lying in bed with feeling ill and so think of labour as a form of illness. Women who lie down also lose some of their sense of competency and can be made to feel 'childlike' by the staff who remain fully clothed and upright.

The experience of childbirth can strengthen a good relationship, bringing the couple closer together and helping them to share the very special magic of the moment of birth. However, it does not magically heal bad relationships, a miracle that many women secretly hope for. Although being present at the birth may help the father to bond to the child in a more intense way than might otherwise have been the case, it will not rebond him to the women, if that primary link has already been broken. Many women believe that if the announcement of pregnancy has not brought their man 'to heel' then being present at the birth will do the trick. They are supported in this hope by the romantic fiction and tabloid newspaper accounts of how playboys become changed men after witnessing their child's birth. Such hopes are often nurtured by women who are, in fact, unhappy within their marriages but 'hoping to make it work'. The baby may be a part of that plan.

Not surprisingly, men and women experience labour and delivery very differently. It happens to the women in an unavoidably personal way and most women have passionate feelings – good or bad – about the experience. Men will tend to talk about it as 'interesting' or 'I'm glad I didn't miss it, I think I learnt a lot', or 'I was really impressed by the whole thing'. They are describing an external event that they have witnessed rather than something which has happened to them. A few men will have 'sympathetic' pains or will seem to have an emotional synchrony with the mother but these may become so wrapped up in their own experience that they are not very supportive to the mother. Understanding that people who love each other may experience even the crucially big events in a relationship quite differently is a very mature attitude. Women are often upset that their partners have such different perceptions of the event and totally different emotional reactions to it.

Again expectations can prove disillusioning or disappointing. Men should try not to expect too much. The bravest woman can have a difficult delivery and soon become bogged down in pain and frustration; the quietest woman may start to swear; the least complaining may suddenly cry and yell. Each woman needs to have a sense of freedom of expression during labour. She needs to know that if she yells, swears, screams, cries, tells dirty jokes because the pethidine has disinhibited her, argues or loses heart, it is not going to be held against her that she is less of a woman than her man hoped she was. If the man cannot cope with such revelations he might do better spending the day with his mates and letting a friend accompany her.

Occasionally men feel uneasy about sexual contact after watching a delivery. 'I was shocked by how much she suffered. I kept thinking that I had done that to her' was one man's description. It is a very basic event physically and for couples who are rather prudish with each other it can make the woman feel too exposed and the husband shocked by what he has seen. The vast majority of men, however, benefit from being present and most say something like 'I wouldn't have missed it for anything.' But women need not be overwhelmed with a need to give their partners this good experience if they have doubts about whether they will find his presence useful. No woman should feel impelled to have any companion that she does not want at such a time. The good of the mother at this point is very directly connected to the good of the child and the health of their future relationship. A happy mother is much more likely to be a good enough mother. Partners, midwives and obstetricians should never let that fact out of their minds during labour.

Labour is not always an uncomplicated event. Even among healthy young women these can be delays and difficulties. All women want healthy babies at the end and most will put up with just about anything to achieve that. I never cease to be amazed at the bravery of women who are determined to have babies. Most of the difficulties are transient and need little intervention to sort out. A forceps delivery, if well carried out, with lots of explanation and good pain relief, should not ruin the magic of the day. It certainly does not represent a failure on the mother's part if she cannot complete the delivery unaided. It usually means that the baby's head was facing in the wrong direction, or that its head was large in proportion to the size of her pelvis, or that there were some signs that the baby was getting tired and needed to come out a bit more quickly.

A minority of deliveries end up as Caesarean sections. In this operation the obstetrician cuts into the abdomen and the utrus to lift the baby out because there is a problem in allowing it to come out by the normal vaginal route. There is some criticism about the number of these operations performed and the criteria used for doing them. Women should have every facility to discuss this operation with their doctors or midwives before the event if there is a reason why it might become necessary. For those who end up having a Caesarian because of a last-minute emergency it is often a distressing and frightening experience because both mother and child are in real danger for a period of time. This experience causes fathers anguish too and can leave the new family feeling very insecure at the start of their lives together. Fathers may blame the baby for almost 'killing' the mother, and some blame the mother for the danger to the baby and the mothers themselves will have all the complications of a massive physical life event, with all the challenge to mental and physical health that implies, over and above the natural trauma of childbirth and early mothering.

It is these mothers who are most at risk of having serious emotional problems in the first year or so after the birth, and this is especially true if it is a first baby. This seems to hold true across a wide social spectrum of mothers and probably means that Caesarean Sections, particularly those undertaken as emergencies, are such large life events that most of us would be overwhelmed psychologically by them. Such women need much support, practical and psychological, while they rebuild their boundaries and recover strength physically. Even six months after the event many report that the psychological after-effects of depression, list-lessness, nightmares and panicky sensations are still with them.

Other deliveries, however traumatic they seem at the time, are not directly related to emotional distress after-wards in such a clear-cut way. This probably reflects that they are significantly less overwhelming as events and the way a woman copes with them depends more on her own resources, the support she gets, the health of the baby and a number of environmental factors. Most women need time to recount the experience a number of times to interested and sympathetic audiences. Even the most normal and least stressful of labours is a big life event in a woman's life and she needs to 'de-brief' over a period of weeks and months to help her integrate that experience among her other memories.

Much work has been done to try and identify the mothers who are most at risk psychologically at or around the time of birth. Sadly, we still have few NHS resources to help such mothers even if we can identify them. Very young mothers can be at special risk and mothers with no social support, particularly those many miles away from their families, are also vulnerable. Women who have unhappy relationships with their own mothers or who have lost mothers through divorce or death before the age of 14 are also more likely to become depressed within a few months of giving birth. There is also a growing number of women who have children later than usual, who have been successful and independent for a number of years prior to the delivery and who tend to be living with or married to equally successful, hard-working (and therefore frequently absent) partners. Such women are at risk of becoming chronically depressed with their lot as mothers and most report that that depres-sion starts rapidly after delivery. If they have also had to have a Caesarean section, something more common in this older group, they may have very high rates of depression. (Interesting work coming from a team in Nottingham sug-gest that moving house or building an extension during the early months is also a further unhelpful factor.) Help, support, warmth and tolerance for these women needs to start from before delivery and be abundant during labour, if they are to have a reasonable chance of adjusting and facing future difficulties.

Labour is the beginning of the long process of separation of child from mother that finally comes to an end when the mother dies (hopefully) many years later. All separations have potential difficulties. Some women report that they do not wish to let go of their child as it is delivered, but most have had enough of pregnancy by this stage and are only too happy to go into labour. There is a need for the mother to recognise during this process that the baby, however dependent, is becoming a separate entity. As with each of the separations that follow this first momentous one, there is an increasing liberty and decreasing responsibility for the mother. Suddenly her body is 'empty' of another and only full of herself again. If she is breast-feeding the sense of togetherness may continue, at least intermittently, for months. However, the transition from being two people to being one is important for mothers to acknowledge themselves. The mothers who refuse to leave their babies with anyone else for days, weeks, even months are denying that this first separation has taken place. The event also begins to mean challenges for the baby who has to gradually understand and come to terms with its own separateness.

Labour is an earthy event. For women who have difficulties with that sense of earthiness it can be experienced as exposing, degrading and humiliating. Many women are embarrassed by exposing their bodies and particularly their genitalia to strangers. This embarrassment is connected to our confusion and ambivalence about female sexuality. The same society which still values virginity, the keeping of a woman's vagina for just one man, also allows pornography to imply that such organs are excitingly available to any man and then expects women to be able to take a 'healthy' attitude towards being exposed during labour. Not surprisingly, women object to the mixed messages about the need to physically 'keep themselves to themselves' and yet remain willing to expose all for 'medical' purposes. In some

Eastern and Islamic cultures such exposure even for health reasons is taboo. Pre-natal classes encourage women to develop a knowledgeable attitude towards their reproductive organs as a way of decreasing anxiety and increasing their sense of control over themselves. If a woman has never looked at her own or any other woman's genitals and would feel appalled by the suggestion that she should, at any time other than in preparation for labour, it is easy to see that exposure to this form of education in mixed groups of prospective parents can be an added stress rather than an aid. Many women report feeling physically degraded by the experience of labour. 'It was like a rape' or 'I shuddered with embarrassment when this young doctor came to do my stitches' are common reflections. Experiencing labour as degrading is often associated with a low self-esteem in the woman, particularly in women who feel confused about their sexuality prior to conception. One doctor told me that she 'almost died of shame' because now that several of her colleagues and her husband had seen her in childbirth they 'know I am a woman'. This was something that she had been trying to hide from herself and them throughout her adult life. She had come from a family where male values were given a great deal more credit than female ones and where her brothers were obviously the favoured children. Her life had been spent trying to win that approval for herself by mimicking their maleness, and childbirth had wrecked her disguise.

Another cause of feeling shame during labour may be external. I am not alone in thinking that many of the people involved in obstetric and gynaecological care do not like or respect women. I think it is possible to hypothesise that they chose such jobs because they are frightened by the power of women – the power to give birth to life – and want to be in positions of power over women in order to reassure themselves. This power can easily be misused and their negative attitudes can all too easily spill over into the way they relate to patients who are in a vulnerable and sensitive state.

Many women would like to believe that pregnancy was not directly connected to sexual activity and that birth was a spiritual rather than physical process. Such beliefs are reflected in many cultures and will also be echoed in the developing psyches of the young child. Children find it notoriously difficult to believe in and accept the sexuality of their parents. If their parents suffer from similar difficulties the relationship between child and parent will be from step one based on false premises. In Chapter 7 we will be looking at how much a woman's view of her sexuality can affect her relationship with her children.

Labour can be a very good memory, but sadly for some women this is not the case. It can be a fruitful beginning to that most intense and difficult of relationships between mother and child, the first step in the lengthy negotiations towards joint separateness. It cannot be forced into any predictable mould. Flexibility is a healthy resource and the more support, understanding and warm acceptance a woman gets at this point in her life the better for herself and the baby.

4

BREAST IS BEST . . . BUT FOR WHOM?

There used to be little choice. Either a baby was breast-fed or it was likely to die. As adults we know that there are now safe alternatives to the breast that are capable of sustaining the baby, but only a few generations ago breast-feeding was a fundamentally important necessity, and failure was a desperate business, sometimes following the death or illness of the mother and often meaning the death of the child too unless an alternative mother-figure could be found. In many parts of the world this desperate need for a mother to be able to feed her baby still exists today.

Babies are very primitive. They have yet to learn about the rules and benefits of our civilisation. They are back at a stage when survival was everything and the desperation with which babies cry for food underlines the ferocity with which they will fight what they perceive as a battle for that survival.

Freud suggested that alongside an urge for life we were all born with an equal and opposite urge for death. As it was difficult, if not impossible, for those two contradictory urges to live inside of one person he decided that the majority of us project the urge towards death outwards onto others. He postulated this theory to explain mankind's aggressive and destructive nature in adult life, and Melanie Klein then extended the concept into childhood as a basis for her understanding of children's psychological development at the breast.

Many later child psychologists have disagreed with this notion, saying that the amount of frustration and dependence experienced by the infant are enough to explain its increasingly aggressive stance as it grows without the need to postulate a death urge. However, all agree that either from birth, or very soon after it, babies are capable of a fiery and destructive rage if frustrated and that this is in some way connected to the individual's need to survive. Each of us has destructive and violent elements to our personalities, however much we may have been taught to hide these or even deny them. Babies have not learnt about hiding the strength of their feelings and so they feel free initially to express themselves without the restraints with which we would normally contain powerful emotions.

As each baby is born with its own personality basis the degree of aggression it experiences and expresses will depend on the baby as well as its environment. As feeding is such a central part of its early experience it is in this arena that the baby's individuality may well express itself first.

Each of us was as totally dependent as our own newly-born babies at the beginning of our lives. However motivated another human being is to fulfilling your needs and providing for your contentment, they will sometimes be slower than you want, and sometimes respond too quickly; they will sometimes give you less than you wanted and sometimes more; they will leave you sooner than you wanted or stay too long. Dependence therefore is bound to be a frustrating experience at times and it is an experience that each parent 'remembers' from their own early days and months of total dependence. Hence the breast-feeding relationship which is the focus of that sensation of dependency is always a complicated relationship.

From the mother's side there is the hope of providing and of caring, hopes that are going to be coloured by her own early feeding experiences as a child. Alongside her need to nurture her baby there will be other psychological needs that may gain supremacy. For instance, mothers who have had difficult relationships with their own mothers, dating back to their earliest days, may want to be especially good mothers themselves. Many women tell me that they have tried hard to be better mothers than their own mothers were. If their own experience of being dependent on their mother was an unhappy and discouraging one, these same mothers may have had to deny their dependency needs very early in life. The baby's dependent demands may reawaken the buried memories both of the mother's failed dependence and of her unmet needs, an acutely painful experience. These mothers may not know why they experience the baby's demands as painful and may feel guilty about those feelings, fearing that they are going to fail to meet the standards they have laid down for themselves. Continuing to meet the baby's demands remains painful for such mothers until they reach an understanding of where the pain is coming from. Some mothers instinctively protect themselves from that psychological pain by becoming less intimate and less reactive to the baby: others may blame the baby by seeing it as too demanding, particularly if it is a girl and therefore identifiable as like themselves.

From the baby's side there is the desperate need to survive, the inevitability of a degree of frustration because of the baby's total dependence, and the potential within the baby for a savage, raging response to such frustration. Alongside of those feelings is the warmth, contentment and feeling of security that appropriate responses of food and closeness produce for the baby. Therefore the feeding experience, even with the best-intentioned mother and the most placid of babies, is a fundamentally good/bad experience.

LEARNING TO BREAST-FEED

Mothers are often made to feel that they are responsible for the success of breast-feeding as if it is something that good mothers know how to do and then enforce on the baby. Like so much of motherhood there is a suggestion that if the mother gets it right the baby will go along unquestioningly with her. As a medical student on a post-natal ward I was taught how to teach new mothers to breast-feed. Equipped with a hazy knowledge of how many pillows were required to achieve this seemingly difficult goal I set out searching for women to help. I found rather desperate young mothers pushing nipples into the mouths of babies that seemed very

bored if not actually asleep. No amount of useful information about organising supportive pillows or expressing
seductive drops of milk induced these babies to suck until
they were ready.

Every baby takes a different amount of time to adjust to
the shock of being born. Women who have received pain-
killers during delivery should not be suprised if their babies
are drowsy initially. Babies can sleep off that drowsiness
just like their mothers and so the women whose babies are
sleepy with medication need not feel any guilt about having
had the medication in the first place. Some seem awake and
aware almost instantly and will often suck immediately
they are put to the breast. Others take several days to wake
up. They are not very interested in anything, including the
breast, during the phase and it is undermining for the
mother so early in this new relationship if she is allowed to
feel that it is her fault in some way. If a baby is healthy it
will start to suck once it is ready. It knows how to suck, it
is even born with a reflex that allows it to turn its head
towards the nipple and suck once it finds it. The baby is programmed for survival in this way. Unfortunately mothers
are not so programmed for emotional survival. Along with
the notion of teaching these mothers how to breast-feed are
other messages about responsibility, and about there being
a right and wrong way to breast-feed. Fingers of guilt about
being a bad mother are entwined within the teaching. If you
were a really good mother, so the myth goes, you would not
need teaching and there would be no problem. And yet all
the mother needs to know is that the baby will teach her to
breast-feed once it wakes up and wants to eat. Only ill or
immature babies who will have difficulties sucking need
special techniques to encourage them.

It is usually the teaching and the expectations that are
wrong rather than the individual mothers, although women
often take the blame for any difficulties and feel they have
to try harder and harder to be the perfect mum. Sadly, many
mothers do not realise that there is such a discrepancy
between what is taught (the ideal) and what they will
achieve (the reality), and so begin to develop mothering
guilt from their earliest days of interacting with their baby.

The majority of babies seem to develop an appetite within a few days of birth and are often enthusiastic about the breast from day four or five. Unfortunately this tends to coincide with the mother experiencing 'baby blues'. There is a well-recognised phenomena of post-operation blues occurring at a similar time interval after any major physical event and so this 'baby blues' reaction is probably not specific to childbirth. It may be the body's way of saying, 'I've had a shock, slow down a bit.'

The baby has, of course, become a reality. It is not the fantasy any longer. As far as the mother is concerned it may not be as wonderful as she had hoped. For instance, many women have a definite sex-preference and the extent of the family's welcome of its new member may also depend on it being the desired sex. Some women have a sense of panic that they will not recognise their babies if separated from them, others yearn to have a few hours' separation from these new and demanding people in their lives. Hence at the same time as the baby becomes interested in eating the mother may feel confused and chaotic about herself, her baby, and their relationship, and the common 'post-trauma' reaction of 'blues' will intensify that confusion.

One of the major problems in mothering is one of timing. Babies and children never want to do things when their mothers want to do them. The reverse is also sometimes true. However much mothers want to respond as reasonable adults to the need of their children, however much they wish to be responsive to the child's sense of timing rather than their own, mothers are only human. If they have just spent three or four days attempting to breast-feed a sleepy and uninterested baby they may well feel rejected and begin to doubt their ability to make this part of the relationship work. Rather than realise that no mother has the ability to make anything work in this relationship without the baby's cooperation they may begin to feel like failures. Then they wake up feeling terrible on day five or six. 'Baby blues' can feel like the end of the world because it is so sudden, often unexpected by the mother, and overwhelming in its nature. Just when they are feeling as if they cannot cope with anything, the baby is suddenly ready to give breast-feeding a go, and may well become furious if that option is not immediately available. Nothing makes breast-feeding fail more rapidly than a mother who is as distraught as her baby at this sensitive time in their new relationship.

Given this scenario it is easy to see why so many mothers rapidly resort to bottle-feeding and tell unhappy tales about this phase of their experience of mothering, and why eating becomes a focus for difficulties within the mother/child relationship for ever. So much of the tension seems to arise from the unreality of the expectations and the detached scientific way in which mothers are taught rather than simply facilitated.

I am impressed by the way new mothers seem to have far less difficulty breast-feeding if they have the early advice and on-going support of someone similar to themselves who is some months or years ahead of them with the same experience. Presumably this is the time-honoured way in which women have facilitated each other for generations. Such knowledge and encouragement should be a sharing experience and not some professional intrusion. In this way a woman can develop a sense of being a normal mother who has normal difficulties and the normal adult need of others to help and share those difficulties. Feeling abnormal, substandard and in need of professional advice to get on with something she feels that she should really be able to do intuitively if she was an adequate mother is the breeding ground for mothering guilt and uncertainty. I have met many mothers who date later difficulties with children, even into teenage years, back to these first days and weeks when they felt they had failed to meet the baby's demands and were thus condemned to fail for ever.

It is important to recognise just how much the early experiences of breast-feeding or bottle-feeding are important in the development of the woman's self-esteem as a mother. If she feels she has failed such an early hurdle she may well become increasingly uncertain of her abilities across the whole spectrum of mothering activities. This will be particularly true if someone important criticises her and sees it as her failure. Mothers-in-law who boast of breast-feeding all their children, husbands who express regret in ways that suggest that they could have done better if given the breasts, friends who suggest that the baby will be psychologically damaged on the bottle, and health care workers who weigh babies and use the results as a measurement of the adequacy of the mothering will all deplete whatever sense of mothering the woman is struggling to gain. Some women are so frightened of failing that they refuse to even give breast-feeding a try, many who continue to breast-feed do so because they know they will feel squashed as mothers if they dare to fail. When asked if they want to breast-feed many women say 'I'll try', perhaps as a way of providing themselves with an escape route from the confusion that can surround the issue if it becomes too intense for them.

PHYSICAL AND PSYCHOLOGICAL PROS AND CONS OF BREAST-FEEDING

Medical advice is that breast-feeding is best for babies because the fat in human milk is more easily absorbed by the baby and this leads to less interference with the absorption of calcium and phosphate which are important for healthy growth. The calorific value of human milk is slightly lower ounce for ounce than dried milk and this is supposed to protect the babies of today from becoming the fatties of tomorrow. The protein content is also lower but they are the right proteins for the baby's growth and include helpful antibodies that the mother has produced and which can protect the baby from infection during the first six months of life. Medically it is also better for mothers in that their bodies regain a pre-pregnant state more rapidly and they continue to lose the weight gained in pregnancy for longer.

Those responsible for giving psychological advice, and many women's support groups, also believe that breast-feeding is best for emotional reasons with both mother and child. It provides the possibility of mother and baby feeling pleased with themselves and each other. Theories talk of mother and baby bonding together during these early days and feeding with all its intimacy is a central part of that bonding. There is much truth in these theories but they are only telling the happy half of the story and ignoring the other angry, difficult and distressing side of this relationship.

If that complete two-sided reality can be accepted by the mother then and only then does breast-feeding truly become an arena for a healthy 'getting to know' each other. Sadly, those mothers who embark on breast-feeding only expecting the happy caring side of the relationship become rapidly discouraged and disillusioned and therefore, despite all these good reasons for continuing, the fact is that the majority of mothers give up breast-feeding within weeks of returning home with the baby.

I think it is important to look at the context in which mothers are having to carry out the advice about the wisdom of breast-feeding because it seems as if however good the advice is in theory the majority of women find it impossible in practice.

One of the basic difficulties for many women is the amount of time it takes to feed the baby itself. This is, of course, seen as a benefit in theory because the more time the mother and baby spend in intimate communication the better. However, it ignores the many other responsibilities mother may have and assumes that she can commit as much time as the baby needs to this one task. If a young baby requires on average between six and eight feeds a day and each feed takes at least 40 minutes the mother is committed to a minimum of 5½ hours' feeding. Mothers with another toddler making demands at the same time often feel guilty about spending so much time with the new baby at the apparent expense of a young child who may well be envious of the baby and its relationship with mother. This becomes increasingly true the more children there are under 5 years old.

I have met many mothers who complain of boredom in spending so much time feeding. 'I felt marooned' was how one mother described the experience of breast-feeding, 'as if I was transported to a desert island for hours each day. Far from making me feel close to my daughter it made me feel increasingly trapped and angry.' Certainly not every woman has the personality to continue this regime without angry and resentful thoughts. This does not mean that they are bad mothers' although often it can be taken as such if they dare to openly express such negative thoughts.

Society is still ambivalent about breast-feeding, despite all the positive messages about its advantages, and therefore it is still a rare sight to see mothers publicly feeding in our culture. Even in small groups among friends many women report either feeling uncomfortable themselves or being aware that they are making others uncomfortable. 'I felt I had to hide away upstairs whenever I was feeding' is a comment I have heard from many women. Usually such inhibitions are restricted to mixed company and are not simply the product of the mother's feelings on the subject, although of course these are also relevant.

Men often feel ambivalent about their partners breast-feeding. This is particularly true of those who see the breast as a sexual object rather than a functional part of another human being. These men often experience jealousy much like the toddler's if they see feeding in progress. Their partners may choose to protect them from such emotions by either feeding out of sight or not breast-feeding at all. In this situation the woman will almost always explain that she was unable to breast-feed rather than suggest any inadequacy in the man.

As that ambivalence between theoretical advice and the reality of the reaction is also present in the outside world women often feel severely limited in what they can do and where they can go when breast-feeding. Even now it is unusual to see mothers breast-feeding while out shopping, or on a family outing. It is certainly not an everyday sight and therefore may well cause people to stare or remark on it. For mothers who feel confident of themselves as women and mothers, this represents much less of a problem than it does for those women who are shy and introverted and care deeply about what other people feel and say about them.

THE WOMAN'S VIEW OF THE SEXUALITY CONNECTED WITH HER BREASTS

Social ambivalence about breasts will not be new to a woman just because she has become a mother. Every woman is exposed to the split between the sexual and the functional aspects of her breasts as soon as they start to develop. Her understanding of her body will depend on her own sense of self-esteem, the messages, overt and covert, she receives from her parents, and the conversations she has with her male and female peers. They will also depend on her sexual experiences prior to motherhood and, at a level deeply buried in her psyche, her relationship with her own mother in the early feeding days of her childhood. For instance, many women who become mothers have been previously abused sexually by father, boyfriend or husband. It is likely that they will have kept the knowledge of such abuse to themselves and carry it around as a confusing and hurtful burden of shame, guilt and anger. Such sexual abuse often involves fondling the breasts and sometimes includes activities that are painful and bruising, both physically and psychologically. For these mothers breast-feeding may remind them of the abuse and cause a return of the desperate emotions they experienced at the time. In such circumstances breast-feeding can become a horrendous nightmare for both mother and baby.

Other women find themselves sexually aroused by breast contact for the first time in their lives by the experience of breast-feeding. This may be either enjoyable or frightening, depending on their understanding of their sexuality. Many women know prior to motherhood that stimulation of the breasts can be pleasurable and are therefore not surprised to find it equally stimulating when feeding as they have previously found it during sexual activity. For fathers this may be a difficult truth to accept however. They do not expect their partners to have a sexual relationship with the baby and the notion that a baby can give the woman pleasure, while the mother is also giving the baby pleasure, may make a man feel jealous and undermined.

Many women therefore keep quiet about their physical experiences while feeding, often not sharing it even with their female friends and relatives. This leaves them uncertain about how normal such experiences are. Many feel that they have become perverted in some way and this is particularly true if their appetite for sexual contact with their man is decreased or even lacking. It is their hidden and sometimes worrying secret. Usually simple reassurance that they are healthy, normal mothers is enough to stop the anxiety but if sexuality is an area of confusion for them anyway, if they feel guilty about not wanting sex with their partners while continuing to be aroused by the baby, or if they have been the victims of real abuse in the past, they will probably need to talk over their thoughts and feelings at some length with a non-judgmental friend, relative or therapist. The vast majority of mothers do not have a forum in which they can explore these issues confidentially. There is often a distressing lack of trust between women which inhibits the sharing of such thoughts with friends or neighbours. These women are isolated with their thoughts which often spill over into dreams and they become increasingly convinced of their own abnormality.

BREAST-FEEDING AND PSYCHOLOGICAL DEVELOPMENT

Stage one: the young baby and the emotionally young parents

Breast-feeding has been given great significance in psychological theories of the development of personality. In order to understand the considerably confused and highly-charged emotions that surround breasts and feeding it is important to understand that it constitutes the most intimate and time-consuming of the many mothering activities of the first year and therefore acts as the most powerful vehicle of emotions between mother and baby. Mothers are not only the providers in this exchange. They and their partners have also been the consumers at some point in their lives and their own experiences will add further depth, sensitivity and possible confusion to the activity.

There are also changing trends of models of breast-feeding. Feeding on demand was advocated as a way of reducing the frustation experienced by babies. Other theorists felt that a four-hourly schedule gave babies a secure and predictable structure to their lives and also taught them to experience frustration within safe limits. Both of these concepts have some theoretical validity but both ignore the issues of the individuality of baby and mother. There is a tendency for such theories to envisage a baby rather as a lump of plasticine that the mother can mould into the desirable shape by her actions, and to assume that all the mother's actions will be consciously controlled and well intentioned. If the baby's psychological shape turns out to be less than desirable it is by implication the mother's fault. Of course, by her actions, her ability to tune into the baby's needs and her ability to respond appropriately to those needs, the mother does teach the baby its first lessons in relating to self and others. Just because the baby is small and looks defenceless, however, does not mean that it is not a partner in the deal. Theories that suggest that the mother is in charge or in control of the situation or can make of it what she chooses not only miss the point but also often encourage a further sense of guilt and failure in the mother unless she can push her baby into whatever the latest psychological trend suggests is healthiest. I think that there is also a more hidden problem for the mothers who do succeed in making themselves and their babies fit the fashion. For them the sense of guilt and frustrations with what they have achieved comes later when whatever trend they followed is repudiated to be replaced by the next. It would be wonderfully liberating to live in an age when women trusted themselves to do what was good enough for their babies without recourse to (usually male) theorists. Certainly the baby is not interested in the theory; she or he is interested in who or what their mother is.

Initially the baby believes itself to be one-and-the-same as the breast. It does not know that the breast is the mother's, but sees it instead as a part of its own body. This is not so surprising considering that the baby has lived inside the mother for nine months and so has been a part of the mother's body for that time. Babies are extremely egocentric initially and, therefore, rather than see themselves as part of the breast, they see the breast as part of them. It is an all-good part of themselves, a part that provides comfort and sustenance, a part that provides a sense of well-being, an antidote to the anxiety that the baby experiences as it begins to suspect that its precious mother is separate from itself.

If the breast or bottle is offered predictably to the baby in response to its needs it begins to develop a sense of being able to control its environment. It can face the growing suspicions about mother's separateness without undue anxiety. However, the relationship is never perfect. There will always be times when the breast is not available in response to the baby's inner needs and therefore the relationship with the breast becomes more contradictory. It is loved when it is fulfilling the needs and hated when it is not. With a growing sense of separateness there is also a growing sense of being dependent on someone or something that is separate. Hence even in the early days of its life the baby's relationship with the breast (and therefore with its mother) is one of profound love on the one hand and raging hate on the other, underlined with the anxiety caused by being dependent on a separate entity which it both loves and hates.

The mother, as a baby, experienced the same confusion and conflict. Her ability to deal effectively with her baby's experience will depend on her own resolution of the difficulties. As we grow we learn that good and bad are part of all relationships and all people, but young babies cannot know that. In those early days they cope with their confusion by conjuring up a good breast (mother) and a bad breast (mother) and believe the two to be separate.

The ability to accept the good and the bad together in each person and in each relationship in life comes with increasing maturity. Some adults maintain the earliest childhood notions of a pronounced split between the two, and our mythology, folk stories and some religions speak of all-good parent figures who are separate from all-bad figures.

For adults who do remain at this split stage of understanding life and relationships are bound to be disappointing and disillusioning. Rather than question their underlying belief in the separateness of good and bad (a belief which protects them from anxiety and confusion), they will start new relationships believing them to be perfect but dismiss them angrily, and often destructively, as soon as they see that the person they love has another contradictory side to their nature. In order to maintain their own sanity such adults often have to believe that they are either completely good and right or completely bad and wrong. It is not unusual for an adult who believs herself to be all-good and right to marry someone who believes himself to be all-bad and wrong. In this way the split they believe to be psychologically true is acted out in their relationship. Although this sounds very painful for the one who believes him or herself to be bad and wrong, most of us place acting out our psychological beliefs more highly than simply being happy. Thus even the 'bad' one gets a sense of confirmation of what they believe to be true from the relationship which they value.

Relating closely to a baby often helps an adult to reconsider his or her own psychological beliefs. Watching our own children struggle with the dilemmas with which we once struggled gives the parent who is involved in the childcare a possibility of reinterpreting themselves and their relationships and coming up with new solutions. Not uncommonly in the good/bad relationship split it is the woman who has accepted the role of the bad, wrong individual. This is partly related to the different values parents ascribe to different sex children from birth, partly related to the differing relationships that men and women have with their fathers and mothers and partly related to the value judgments of the outer world of business, economics and politics that suggest that maleness as a stereotype is more culturally acceptable and right. Adults who have accepted a bad, wrong position in this fundamental split have much more motivation to change that view of themselves if a psychological opportunity to do so is offered than do those who believe themselves to be all right. Motherhood may well offer such an opportunity for women with previously low self-esteem, who learn by interrelating with their children that they are different people to the ones they have always believed themselves to be.

As one such woman said to me, 'I could hardly believe it when I realised that my baby loved me and then I felt very sad because I realised that it was the first time I had been loved like that. I hated it when the baby cried. I felt so bad, that familiar sense of being all wrong. But then the baby would smile. I found that I could make the baby happy and he responded to me with smiles and curled his body into mine as I cuddled him. I knew for the first time ever that something I was doing in a relationship was all right and that another human being was acknowledging something good from me and something all right inside of me.' What this woman was describing so movingly was her own sense of learning to merge the good and the bad within herself, alongside of the baby showing by his reactions that he perceived her as both. It is not uncommon for mothers to learn new and fundamental things about themselves in this early intense relationship with a feeding baby. Sadly, the father in this family was less exposed to the baby in these early feeding moments and therefore could not learn from them in the same way as the mother. The basis for their marriage had been a covert understanding that she was to blame for all their problems, leaving him guiltless and above reproach, even though to an outsider he seemed very demanding and unreasonable. They had been emotionally young adults prior to becoming parents. With the baby's help she rapidly began to grow psychologically while he tried with increasing desperation to maintain the status quo.

This is a common situation and often leads to separation and divorce within a few years of starting to parent together. It represents a good reason for parents to engage in the basic activities of parenting equally so that they have equal opportunities to grow in psychological understanding. That experience will increase their feelings of mutual support and understanding rather than allowing the unbridgeable gulf that so often occurs in marriages at this early stage of parenting.

It is impossible always to be right as a parent (and sometimes with a baby who cries for no apparent reason it feels impossible to ever do anything right at all). The parents who interpret their experiences in relationships in black/white, good/bad terms, and believe that all their own problems stem from the outside world, will find it hard to cope with the rage of a small baby; she or he will either blame the other parent or the baby. So a father may consider the woman inadequate because their baby cries too much for his own psychological comfort or he may decide that there is something wrong with the baby for it to behave in that way. This may lead to repeated trips to the family doctor demanding that something be done for the 'sick' child despite the fact that the parent is told that the baby is normal and healthy.

If a crying child is not considered ill by such a parent it may be considered to be naughty, badly disciplined and in need of punishment. Parents who abuse alcohol are particularly prone to make such an assumption and act out on it, but many other parents begin to hit or even torture their babies in the belief that this will make them behave better. For such a parent 'behaving better' means a baby behaving in a way that does not produce psychological stress in the parent. Once the parent starts to experience distress, blame is immediately attributed to the 'bad' baby who the parent then punishes. Such punishment usually leads to the baby becoming increasingly unhappy and demanding for a time, leading the parent to increasing levels of violence. After a while the baby becomes subdued and quietly distressed. At this stage the violence may cease, leaving a baby both physically and emotionally scarred for ever. In some families the circle of violence is such that once a baby has been identified by the abuser as a 'bad' baby the punishment continues even once the baby is quiet. In this situation the parent is psychologically as young as the child, having become 'stuck' at the earliest stage of splitting the good and the bad and then projecting one or other aspect out of themselves and into their closest relationships.

We all know that babies and small children can be the victims of terrible abuse and each year a number are killed. Whenever we hear about this on the news we wonder how such a thing is possible and yet each of us who has had responsibility for an infant night after night has felt like exploding and doing something violent at points of great stress. As feeding is often the focus of both parental stress and baby's difficult demands, the babies who have difficulty establishing a pattern of feeding and the parents who feel less than capable are especially at risk of escalating rage within both baby and parent. It is important that these parents understand that they are quite different psychologically to those who are responsible for the gross abuse we hear about on the media. To feel frustrated, angry, at the end of your tether, and as if you will explode are all normal experiences of parenting. To act out such feelings and to believe that the 'bad' baby is responsible for your behaviour is the abnormal and immature response to that normal experience.

The vast majority of parents do not batter or torture their babies when they feel like this, although many will admit to being fearful that they might. Usually the parents who come to a helping agency saying that they are worried about hurting their children are those at the over-controlled end of the spectrum who are aware of their rage and feel desperately ashamed of having such feelings. Many are already feeling like failed parents who need reassurance about their own normality and capabilities rather than criticism. They may need practical help to cope with a baby's demands either because their own resources are limited or because that particular baby is unusually demanding. These parents are also psychologically young and tend to see themselves as the 'bad' parents rather than attribute any responsibilities for their problems to the baby.

Breast-feeding in either situation (either the split good/bad parents who sees the baby as 'bad', or the one who splits just as much but sees herself as 'bad' instead) may be too much of a strain when added to other psychological burdens. It may be preventing the woman from getting any rest and physically debilitating her. Often these mothers are so frightened by what they see as their inadequacies that they hardly dare to give up breast-feeding. They may feel they have no right to ask for help and see the baby as totally their responsibility. Such self-denying mothers are martyring themselves to their task. They often feel resentful and explosive inside and yet will hold off all attempts of others to help until they are literally on their knees with fatigue. Then if they do explode, sometimes towards the baby but more usually at themselves, they cannot forgive themselves and often seek punishment for many years afterwards.

Such mothers often had unsatisfactory relationships with their own mothers. These relationships also started to go wrong back at the early stage of feeding experiences. The women may feel superficially that they love their mothers and yet be highly competitive with them. As one woman explained to me, 'My mother was too vulnerable to fight her or hurt her and so I got my own back by being much better than her. Whatever she had suffered or put up with I wanted to prove that I could take even more and then still be a better mother to my kids.' Their belief that they have no right to ask for help may well date back to early experiences with a mother who could not respond to their demands for food and comfort adequately. Instead of learning to rage and to see the mother as inadequate or her circumstances as unreasonable the daughter believes that her demands must be too great. She learns from these early experiences that she should not make demands, that she is not entitled to that loving and caring for which she continues to yearn psychologically. However difficult such mothers find the reality of mothering they often find asking for support even harder and will only do so when they can cope no further.

In many ways it is easier for helping agencies to deal with mothers who get into feeding difficulties because of their own psychological limitations than for them to deal with the limitations of partners or social circumstances. As it is easier to deal with mothers, such agencies tend to look for and apportion blame to the mother primarily and will only seek to find other reasons for the problems if pushed. Clinics tend to see mothers with their babies while health visitors and social workers can call round to see those mothers who do not attend or seem to be having particular difficulty. Often it is much more difficult to get to see a father. Many of the tensions in homes originate around the father and his behaviour, however, and without view of him it is difficult to offer sensible help. These men feel resentful that help is being offered by people they see as 'interfering'. The people who wish to help may well be as intimidated by such fathers as their partners often are, and therefore choose to deal with the mothers for their own safety. Often violent or difficult fathers have themselves seen the levels of alcoholism or violence in their own families that they then descend to. They may consider their behaviour normal. They may feel that they have a right to behave as they wish within their own homes. The women who live with such men are often also the products of violent homes. They are unlikely to complain directly about the behaviour even when they are being regularly assaulted.

The arrival of a small baby into such a home immediately raises the emotional temperature. The baby with its demands will rock an already unstable boat. Such mothers tend to be quite different to the over-controlled martyring mothers who bring attention to their own fears of damaging the baby. Instead these mothers will rather tend to deny and hide any damage or difficulties in order to protect their men. They share the difficulties of breast-feeding safely, however, because images of breast-feeding are so highly charged with negative as well as positive emotions that even if the mother can manage with her own emotions amidst such chaos, she may well be igniting a fierce and vengeful jealousy and rage in her violent man which will result in danger to both mother and baby. Some mothers stand between these men and their children, taking much physical abuse in an attempt to protect the children, but many mothers are beaten beyond resistance or courage and may even feel a sense of relief that the man's violence is temporarily aimed at the children rather than themselves.

Hence, although breast-feeding is seen as best for physical and psychological reasons, the limitations of the woman's psyche and her environment must be taken into account. Far better not to enrage a potentially violent husband, not to overstretch a vulnerable woman, not to overload the mother with many other commitments and not to stir the embers of past sexual abuse of sexual confusion if this can be avoided with bottle-feeding. Many mothers therefore choose this alternative not because they are rejecting established advice but because they know better about themselves, their past, their abilities, and their present situation than any professional. Sadly, many women still feel guilty about a choice even if it is made for the wisest of reasons.

Equally sadly bottle-feeding does not necessarily alleviate any of the above problems either. Hence these women may have made a wise choice in the hopes of keeping the emotional temperature cooler for themselves and others only to find that the baby's relationship with the bottle can be every bit as heated and difficult as that with the breast. The bottle is not a predictable panacea and any feeding situation can be potentially explosive given the wrong mixture of adult and baby feelings. The important thing to remember in such a situation is that the baby is involved in the relationships and the reactions even though it is not responsible for them.

Stage two: the baby and parents grow towards accepting limitations

As the baby grows and its awareness of its surroundings increases, it will attempt to control more and more of what goes on around it. As it realises that mother is separate it has several psychological choices. It can accept that discovery and get on with its exploration of relationships acknowledging separateness as a basis for its exploration of others, it can sink into an infantile sadness which is a form of grief over the loss of being merged with mother, or it can fight to maintain as much closeness as possible with mother. Most babies fight a little, grieve a little and get on with learning about relationships too. If they are tired or ill they will demand to be back very close to mother, whatever else is going on and whoever else needs her. If they experience a need to re-establish that closeness they will not, for instance, take mother's fatigue or inability to respond into account. They will simply experience their own needs and act accordingly. Their future responses to the same situation depend on a complex interaction that then occurs between mother and baby. The mother needs to decide on the appropriateness of the baby's demands given its age, its present state, and her own resources. Hence, if she has just decided to wean the baby from the breast because she feels tired and fed up with such feeding, and she has reason to think that the baby is fighting that decision about a form of increased separation, she has to weigh her fatigue against the baby's perception of its needs.

That negotiation between the mother's increasing need to separate and regain her own sense of self and the baby's need to keep her as close as possible, therefore denying the fact that they are separated, is a key feature of the first years of life. Often the negotiation is centred around food. I have known a few mothers continue to breast-feed into the child's fourth year and very occasionally even longer. Such mothers represent the far end of this negotiation. Other mothers decide to introduce solid foods much earlier than advised and seek to make the baby more independent about feeding as quickly as possible. Usually these far ends of the spectrum represent the mother's emotional needs rather than the baby's and the closer you get to the middle of the spectrum the more likely this is to be the result of a negotiation of some sort.

All negotiations are about power, bluff and double-bluff, rejected and accepted offers, and only the most successful leave both parties feeling that they have won. Negotiations about feeding are just the same. Some mothers feel adequately powerful to make a plan of feeding, breast or bottle, and then of weaning, and stick to it. Other mothers feel quite powerless and that they have to give in to the baby on most occasions. Some mothers are very flexible in their plans, others very rigid. Bluff and double-bluff often reflect the players' levels of confidence. Babies can be very strong players indeed especially if they sense that opposition is beginning to crumble. I have never ceased to be amazed at the extraordinary ability of babies to yell, cough, go red in the face and gasp for breath with fury if they think that there is something to be gained in this way. If they sense that this time mum has won they will quite suddenly change their minds, and drop blissfully into sleep, usually with perfectly contented smiles playing on their previously very angry lips.

This represents the second stage of personality development. Having firstly separated out the good and bad mother and then having had enough intimacy with the good mother to control anxieties about separation, the baby then becomes faced with the reality of separation. It cannot be put off for ever and it is in the manner of its feeding that it probably first begins to experience changes. A mother's experience of separation will influence her ability to help the baby come to terms with this reality in relatively good humour. However, there is a fundamental sadness apparent in many babies as they realise that the 'good old days' of getting just about everything you want when you want it are over for ever. Many peole go on believing that if they are good enough, clever enough to find the right relationship in later life that the sense of being inseparable from the source of comfort, food and warmth will return. Rather like the adults who remain for ever at the stage of splitting good and bad, those who stay permanently hopeful in order to avoid the finality of the separation are also bound to be disillusioned with life and future relationships. That extraordinary closeness which each of us experiences *in utero*, and most of us continue to experience for several more months and even years after birth, is bound to be lost as the baby grows towards becoming a separated and more independent child. The cost of not giving up that closeness would be lifelong dependency. The adults who do get stuck at such a stage tend to become depressed more easily than most by life. They sense that they are dependent on others and are often angry about that dependence, particularly when the person they are dependent on lets them down in some way.

A mother will tend to use her own coping mechanisms to help the baby through this difficult phase. We all have a range of mechanisms that allow us to keep the impact of events and relationships within bearable limits for our own peace of mind. For the most part these defences are a useful part of our psyche that allow us to get on with day-to-day life without being overwhelmed by its inevitable difficulties. Sometimes the defences become too rigid and then they become increasingly a problem in their own right. The most common mechanism is denial. We can stare at a problem but say to ourselves 'this is not a problem' or 'this may be problem for others but not for me'. Mothers can communicate this attitude to a baby they are attempting to feed, or burp, or wean. It is often very reassuring for the baby to know that the sensations it is experiencing do not worry its mother at all. It can then grow up to deny similar small issues and feel unworried by them.

There is a form of mania that we all use from time to time to deal with sadness about loss. We usually call it humour. The mothers who themselves depend on humour to survive the rigours of life will also put energy into making their babies laugh when they look as if they might otherwise burst into tears. They will play peek-a-boo, tickle them or blow on their tummies to produce that gurgling laughter that is so attractive from babies. For the baby who is experiencing sadness or fury at being weaned, such mothers make food into a game: the spoon becomes an aeroplane, for instance. Different food may have different noises. In this way the humorous mother is teaching the baby to associate the difficult feelings with other happier feelings. Such babies will then tend to conjure up amusement later on in life when they are similarly depressed. They will, in effect, be learning, via the medium of coping with changes in eating and all that it implies in closeness with mum, how to survive in later life emotionally.

A third popular form of coping is to displace attention from the baby's inner world of discontent to something fascinating or pleasing in the outside world. Even very young hungry babies can be distracted for a few minutes with songs, being cuddled, and some bright stimuli. As a baby grows its potential for using the outside world as a distraction from the inner world increases.

Used creatively and within reasonable limits such coping defence mechanisms are important. In order to be able to communicate them mother and baby need to have a relationship which makes a healthy vehicle for emotional contact between them. Early feeding difficulties often reappear when separation is in view in the form of weaning. This is why it is so important for all those mothers who consider themselves early failures to have had enough positive strokes themselves by this time to re-establish their sense of competency.

MOTHERS' NEEDS DURING BREAST-FEEDING

In order to be able to cope with the emotions that breast-feeding will arouse in her baby and herself a woman needs to feel secure in the immediate family world that surrounds her. During both pregnancy and labour the woman's sense of having personal boundaries, both physical and psychological, has been breached. This allows for a form of closeness with the baby that is unique in human relations but the closeness is achieved at the cost of the mother maintaining her boundaries at a decreased level. The normal defences she uses on a daily basis to protect herself from hurtful comments or difficult situations in life are at an all-time low in order to allow the baby psychological access to her. At this time a feeding mother is rather like a country that has disarmed unilaterally and then finds itself under attack from both inside and outside. Without her own defence mechanisms to block them, memories, pains, fears and traumas come flooding back to her. Many women talk of an increase in dreams, more vivid and frightening content and more intense accompanying emotions. For some these dreams will bring back events from the past long forgotten, for others they will be terrifyingly twisted versions of the day-to-day experience of the here and now. For instance, one woman, who had been in a foster home for several weeks as a toddler, saw repeated images of the foster parents' faces sweeping towards her in a menacing way in her dreams when her own baby was four weeks old. 'I don't know whether I am coming or going,' she said. 'I'm exhausted and dying for a good sleep on the one hand and yet frightened that as soon as I drop off they will be there.' Gradually, over a period of several weeks, her memories of those few weeks began to return to her and she realised that she had been very unhappy and frightened that her parents had left her for ever. She was able to go back and discuss this incident with her parents, both of whom had been injured in a crash when she was very young, necessitating the weeks in foster care. They remembered that she had been sent there without any explanation of why or for how long, and that when she came home she was withdrawn and obviously unhappy for many weeks. As the mother said, 'It was like a scene of a play lighting up and I suddenly understood my feelings towards Anna (the new baby) as well as the dream. I had been frightened to let Anna out of my sight. I wanted her to know we would never go away. I had even told my husband we could never have a babysitter and he was really fed up with me. After talking with my parents I began to be able to let go a little without feeling sick and anxious.'

Emotions that have been defended against for many years will surface in new mothers who are engaged in feeding their babies. Many women comment that they have never felt as angry as they do with their babies. Some women become overwhelmed with a sadness that they have ignored previously. Women who have had a major loss during their lives, particularly the loss of a mother, will start to grieve as if the loss is fresh as a rush of emotions burst through the depleted defences. Anxieties, sadness, rage, jealousy, envy, hate and love all come bubbling up from the individual woman's mind. As we live in a culture that encourages as to repress these feelings all the time, it can be a frightening experince for both the woman and the adults close to her to realise that such emotions lurk within. It is important to remember that they lurk within us all, but feeding small babies is an especially powerful releasing agent. Babies have this range of powerful feelings towards us and that may act as a catalyst to our own submerged emotions. Also, fatigue and long-term sleep deprivation are known to affect psychological boundaries dramatically.

For the mother who is psychologically flexible it is possible to be relatively defenceless with the baby, especially when feeding, but to increase her defences at other times. This sort of flexibility takes practice, however, and it is usually only achieved after a period of trial and error. Hence, at least during the early weeks, the mother will feel and be psychologically open to any assault on herself, as well as feeling physically vulnerable. This form of emotional vulnerability lasts for as long as the close and intimate nature of breast- or bottle-feeding continues. It is a state in which women are at psychological risk and should therefore be protected from unnecessary attacks. This is not always what happens however. Often they are thrown back into the whirlwind of life, poverty, housing difficulties, mortgages, looking after other children and dealing with their husbands, friends, families and colleagues within a matter of days. In this situation women have to make choices about how they survive. If they continue in a defenceless way to enhance mother/baby bonding they may do so at enormous emotional cost to themselves. If they regain their defences then the new relationship may suffer instead. There is no right or wrong in this most personal of equations, only the not-so-gentle battle of compromise fought out in the painfully unprotected grounds of early motherhood. Other involved adults who are not in this vulnerable state can help or hinder, however, and we will be looking at the role of the father and the larger family later in the book.

In summary then, breast-feeding is agreed to be theoretically best for mother and baby, from both physical and psychological standpoints. In reality few mothers follow this advice for longer than a few weeks because they are living in environments, and within relationships, especially those with partners and other children, which make that theoretical advice impractical. Many women find that they need to be able to control the distance between themselves and their babies because of their own psychological response to this, the earliest the most ambivalently heated, experience of mothering. Any form of feeding will leave women depleted and vulnerable and they will therefore need extra support and acceptance to survive psychologically. There is, however, the very positive long-term gain of being able to view the world of babyhood again through the eyes of our own child, look at ourselves in fresh colours and grow psychologically almost as fast as the well-fed child will grow physically. There is a great deal of grey and very little black and white about the rights and wrongs of feeding. The vast majority of mothers do what is necessary for the infants' physical survival, and it is rather in the area of psychological health that difficulties can occur. Generally speaking the mother who knows and accepts herself, limitations and all, and who has made the two crucial steps ((a) recognising the good and bad in all people and relationships, including herself and her relationship with the baby's father, and (b) coping with the separateness that exists in even the closest relationships) in psychological development herself will help a baby through the rigours of infanthood and towards capable childhood more effectively than the saints, martyrs or villains – those adults who remain 'stuck' at an early age psychologically and who may be as young as the baby in emotional terms.

5

PROBLEMS AND PRIVILEGES OF THE WORKING MOTHER

All mothers work. Some choose to work for their husbands or partners and children full-time. For this they receive their board and keep and whatever else they are capable of negotiating. They do not receive an income and their position offers a very partial security, both for themselves and their offspring. This work is usually seen as a twenty-four-hours-a-day, seven-days-a-week job, with no predictable time off. Most women who choose this route will say that they labour in this way because they love their family and want to give their efforts wholeheartedly to them. Some are embarrassed by this choice, the 'I'm only a housewife' syndrome, while others are staunch supporters that their chosen way is the best way to be both wife and mother. Until recently the majority of wives of middle- or upper-class husbands would not expect to work after marriage. Being able to quit their jobs in the 'outside' world to take up their roles in the 'inner' world was seen as the perk of marrying 'well'. Many husbands would find it insulting to their own capabilities to earn for their families if such wives demonstrated any enthusiasm for working themselves during their marriage. The comment 'surely she doesn't need to work' is usually a comment to reassure the world that he is capable of providing all they need, and not a comment that reflects his wife's personal needs.

Many other women go out to work as well as work within the family. For some this is a matter of choice and may even feel like a luxury at times. For many others it is an economic or socal reality. In the recent unemployment crisis in the UK it has been easier in many areas for women than men to find work. This is usually because women will work longer and harder for less financial reward than men and are therefore employed in preference. Although most of our social conditioning, television, papers, books and plays still depict the wife and mother in the home, the majority of women with children over 5 now work at least part-time outside the home as well.

Very few paid working women can afford completely to replace their input to their homes, partners and children. Indeed most do not want to because then there would be little point in having families in the first place. However, there is a difficult balancing act they need to achieve of being able to replace enough of themselves in one situation in order to function effectively or even survive in both. Women who go out to work generally have troubles allowing themselves to be adequately replaced and these difficulties are only partially financial or practical. Undoubtedly for some women the lack of nursery provision, coupled with their partners' unwillingness to undertake regular household tasks and/or responsibility for their children, is a major practical stumbling block to adequate self-replacement. However, the same syndrome exists to much the same extent among professional women with significantly higher salaries and greater freedom in how they choose to cover their various roles, suggesting that women have an underlying problem in allowing replacement help into their homes.

This underlying problem revolves around a woman's sense of competition with other women. The image of the au pair seducing the husband is commonplace. Women worry that a 'motherly' second figure in the home will insert herself into the wife position and become increasingly attractive to the husband, who will come to see the hired help as the main female figure of the house. Of course such situations do occur and I know many women who joke (but very seriously) that making sure the help is ugly is their major criteria in selection. This is usually the competitive anxiety of a woman who has not worked outside the home for many years because women who are familiar with the outer working world know only too well that their partners' opportunities for seducing and seduction in the open market place are certainly no less than at home.

The second competition anxiety is usually a much more difficult hurdle, however, because it involves the woman's sense of being the most important person in her child's eyes. Mothers, especially with first children, feel sensitive about their abilities to 'mother'. Those returning to work after maternity leave do so after between three and six months of getting to know the baby, and often still feel relatively incapable as a mother. They fear that the caring figure who replaces them will seduce their baby away from themselves. Of course there is some truth in this supposition. A baby will respond to a regular caring adult in its environment and many of the women who go into careers as child-minders, nannies and mothers' helps undoubtedly do have a streak of competition with the real mother. This fear is surprisingly strong in many of the working mothers I have spoken to, although they are often embarrassed and ashamed to admit it.

Paula, 24, high-flyer in the business world with a baby of 9 months said, 'Every day I went home to find the nanny and the baby happy and relaxed, and then five minutes after she had gone home the baby and I were in tears.' This situation rapidly became distressing enough for Paula to seek help and guidance. Should she stop work? Was she a career woman who could not be a satisfactory mother? Should she listen to her family, and in particular her husband, who became increasingly critical of her job during this phase? I suggested we took one step back from these questions to look at what was actually happening and to talk to the people involved. Paula worked from 8.30 a.m. to 4.30 p.m. and had three-quarters of an hour travelling each way. Occasionally she had to go away on business trips overnight but on these occasions her husband made special efforts to be home early to put baby Stella to bed.

Against some opposition from Paula I suggested that I should meet with all three of the major carers, herself, her husband John, and Margaret, their 23-year-old nanny.

Within the first five minutes of our meeting I discovered that this was the first 'triangular' meeting they had had since hiring Margaret six months earlier. Margaret left whenever the first parent to get home arrived and therefore had no opportunity to talk to both.

Paula explained how bad she felt the situation had become and said that she was thinking about giving up work because she felt the tension was bad for Stella and herself. I asked her to describe exactly what was wrong to both Margaret and John. She talked about the first hour of her homecoming each evening with the tears, frustrations and feelings of helplessness. I asked John what his experience of homecoming was, to which he replied that he made a point of not getting home before 6.30 or 7.00 these days in order to miss 'the fuss'. I asked what happened when he had to be home early if Paula was away. At this point Margaret intervened with 'I always make sure that Stella is fed, washed and changed early on those days.' There was a loud silence in the room after she had spoken. John said bashfully, 'I was just about to say that I think I cope rather well.' It also then became clear that when John was caring for Stella, Margaret would stay for half an hour or so after he got home to allow him time to have a cup of tea and a quiet read of the paper before taking over responsibility for Stella.

It had not occurred to any of the three that Paula was under similar pressures in the outside world to John and also arrived home tired and often fed up. Margaret had responded 'naturally' to that need in John for some brief peace between the outer and inner world and he had 'naturally' accepted that caring from Margaret without any sense of having to immediately put himself at Stella's disposal. The two-way interaction between Paula and Margaret was quite different. Paula often hurried home and wanted to take over caring for Stella as soon as she came into the house. 'I feel guilty about being away from her all day,' she said, 'and I feel that I have to spend every minute of my time at home looking after her.'

At this point Margaret said that although she knew her job depended on Paula working and that therefore she recognised her feelings as perhaps unreasonable in the circumstances, she had very different feelings to John going out to work when Stella was still so young to those she had for Paula. 'I wouldn't leave a baby that young myself,' she asserted.

'Do you think that Paula is a bad mother?' I asked Margaret.

She felt confused and threatened by such a straight-forward question and it is a tribute to her honesty and ability for personal reflection that she eventually replied, 'I wouldn't say bad exactly, just not like me.'

It is an obvious but rarely discussed fact that women who choose to work outside the home must be different to those who choose paid employment within the home. From an observation point (although often not when engaged in the relationship) it is equally obvious that these differences can lead to misunderstandings, envy and criticism. These emotions are usually two-way. Women who are paid for child-care often care with a similar intensity of feeling to the mother, at least in the short term. This is lucky for the many children who rely on their care but difficult for both women involved.

There is a need for mother and mother-substitute to talk together and explore their sense of competition over the rights and wrongs of baby-care. The mother needs to remember that she is the employer and has rights in that position. Equally she needs to bear in mind that child-care is a highly personal business which most people conduct to their own best abilities when left to do it their way. Good child-minders and nannies can accept that they sometimes feel critical and competitive, and are able to put those feelings into the context of the highly-charged and confusing relationship between two women who 'share' the care of a baby. The competition is usually a mirroring for both women of the relationships they have had with their own mothers and we will be discussing this further in Chapter 8.

What of the father caught in the middle of this competitive relationship? John's experience is not so unusual. Fathers are often treated more caringly by the mother-substitute than their partners, and are usually unaware of the discrepancy and surprised when it comes to light. Most men are also unaware of the ferocity surrounding inter-female competition, especially where mothering is concern-ed, and may therefore be unknowingly seduced, either by the mother into thinking that the mother-substitute is bad, or vice versa. Given that the paid working mother with a young child is under considerably more stress and usually much more fatigued than the mother-substitute, who is usually only doing that one job as opposed to the mother's two, it is easy for a mother's sense of competence to be worn away and for a man to find himself colluding in that process of erosion rather than supporting his tired, hard-working partner. Most men do not have the experience of mothers who worked themselves, and will also therefore have expectations about what 'proper' mothers do that bear no resemblance to the way in which paid working mothers simply have to manage. We will be looking at these expecta-tions in more detail in Chapter 7.

Alongside the competitive aspects of sharing the care of your children with another woman there is the deeply-rooted guilt of not being there yourself to provide the care. I know of few women who will say they have never experienced at least some guilt in this situation. This guilt stems from doing something that is different to cultural stereotypes, different to the pattern of the lives of parents, and different to what much of their peer group regard as the right and proper way to behave. There is an underlying cultural assumption that women have to be self-denying in order to help their men and children survive and prosper. I have often heard groups of women competing over who is the most self-denying. They measure their success as adults by their degree of achieved martyrdom and may be highly critical of any woman who does not meet their own perverse standards. Women who have stayed at home to care for children and hated the experience are also often fiercely critical of a generation of women who have had more freedom of choice about the issue.

Many mothers who go out to work face regular criticism from relatives, friends and colleagues, especially when their children are pre-school age. If and when things go wrong the phrase 'well, his mother works' is often proffered as an explanation. Relatives can be particularly cruel to working mothers because they are unlikely to be as openly critical and tend to disguise their opinions in over-solicitousness about the child, which is bound to feed the mother's own sense of worry about the child's welfare. Comments from relatives that fall into this category include from one mother-in-law the inquiry on one visit as to whether the 'maid' starved the baby as it was looking thin, and then, only four weeks later, whether the baby was being properly weaned because it seemed rather bloated; there was the uncle who would say on every visit, 'Well, the children *seem* to be relatively well adjusted!' and the mother who, while apparently encouraging her daughter to succeed, would walk around the baby's room running her fingers along the furniture and talking loudly about dust mites. They tend to be comments that the new mother finds hard to recognise instantly as critical, but rather leave her with an uncomfortable feeling of increasing anxiety about the baby's welfare and about whether she is being as responsible as the family think she ought to be.

These attacks on the paid working mother come out of confusion, genuine anxiety about the baby or the father's welfare, inappropriate anxiety based on the relatives' own experience of parenting, envy, hostility and psychological theories about children who are separated from their mothers becoming psychopaths or depressives. Such theories were rife in the early post-war years. Women were forced home to rear families and look after their menfolk by such dire warnings that represent a considerable distortion of the original observations and reports by men such as Bowlby and Winnicott. Children who are placed in care from already disturbed families to impersonal institutions at an early age, who suffer from multiple handling and little genuine warmth or interest undoubtedly do suffer emotionally both at the time and later in life. The notion that in order to avoid such damage mothers needed to spend the first five years of their children's lives glued to their sides was an illogical and damaging reaction to these early observations on deprived children. Indeed I am becoming more and more certain that it is impossible for one adult, however mature and well intentioned, to give a child a balanced, healthy upbringing. The mother may be essential but that should not be confused with being universal. Most mothers have definite limits, and there are emotions, experiences and knowledge which they cannot impart to their children because they do not have it themselves. We have known this for centuries about intellectual education, but emotional education is just as important for the growing person and is often neglected not by design or purpose, not from lack of love or good intention, but because of lack of love in the mother's upbringing, lack of resources in her present environment, and fatigue and stress. The mothers who hang on to the notion that they can be the total providers of the best psychological environment for their baby and toddler probably do themselves and their children no favours.

Every mother wants to have influence over the baby and its upbringing. Every mother has the ability to provide something which is precious and unique for that baby within the context of her relationship with it. Every mother has limits, physical, intellectual, emotional and spiritual. Every baby has much to gain from other caring adults: the father, the grandparents, friends, extended family and paid child-carers. At the present time there is no evidence to suggest that a mother working in any capacity adversely affects the child's psyche or their relationship, although there is some suggestion that poverty, unintelligence, lack of education and emotional deprivation in the parents can all do damage. Although there has been little detailed research work, most paid working mothers think it common sense to replace themselves with someone they trust and like as the second major care-giver to their children. Historically, for all but the richest strata of society, this was probably a mother, aunt or close friend. Nowadays it is more likely to be a paid care-giver, the vast majority of whom make excellent part-time replacements for the woman who goes out to work.

Despite this all working women will be able to tell you of various horrendous experiences they have had with the 'paid help'. In particular, those who rely on untrained or inexperienced young women tend to have unfortunate and hair-raising experiences. Such experiences are more likely to cause stress, anguish and anxiety to the parents than harm the children however. Children are very resilient to the ups and downs of their various care-givers as long as their central relationship with their mother remains consistent. It is this important fact which the guilt-ridden, anxious and competitive new mothers who want to work should try to remember. Their relationship with the baby is unique and central to both the baby and themselves. Many other adults will add to the richness of the baby's environment but none will give the baby quite the sense of security that it has with its original point of attachment, namely mum. Hence the heavy responsibility that lies with that mum, whether she is there or not in person, and the knowledge that the baby will save the real intensity of its love and its hate, its security and its fears for her.

I vividly remember visiting my youngest son in hospital after an operation on his middle ear. As I sat on the bed, he sat up and vomited all over me. 'He's been saving that for you,' commented the nurse as she raced past. How often the vomit, the tears, the fury and the need for a cuddle are saved up until mum comes home we never know. To a busy, fraught working mum it seems fairly commonplace to open her front door onto varying scenes of chaos with which she then is expected to cope. I often think it is a family's way of testing the mum to see just how capable she is. Perhaps it helps to see this as testing rather than a passively aggressive way of demonstrating their belief that mum should be constantly available at all hours of the day and night.

Whatever the job and however long the hours, mothers who go out to work have to develop a series of priorities. There are some situations which demand their attendance and attention in both spheres of their lives and they need to be able to weigh up those demands and respond in ways that they can later justify to themselves, their children and others. It helps to have given some thought to this balance before the disaster strikes, although the combination of job and motherhood manage to throw up some extraordinarily difficult situations which most of us would never have dreamt of prior to their occurring. There are the obvious clashes of responsibility . . . what do you do if the child is ill and there is an important event at work? . . . what do you do when the child-minder's children have measles and you have not had measles and work with other children? . . . how do you plan for the unforeseen emergency, the accident or the appendix, if your job takes you out and about without warning? The list is endless and each parent has to find their own priorities for the situation, the child and themselves. Generally speaking it reduces anxiety if the child-minder has already discussed with the mother what approach they should take to temperatures, sore throats, apparent sore ears, stomach upsets and accidents. The child-minder should have the number of the child's GP, as well as many ways as possible of contacting both parents, and grand-parents, too, if necessary. Particularly for the inexperienced and young carer, an hour or two on how to deal with most common household accidents is not wasted, along with an intimate knowledge of where to find antiseptic, plasters and whatever else the child may require. Knowledge is a great reducer of anxiety on both sides and the child will feel more secure whatever the problem if the adult looks as if they know what they are doing. I have seen a number of parents after their child has been involved in an accident, usually not very serious, when they were not around. The sense of shock is compounded with guilt, and often fierce anger either with the carer or the child or both. This reaction occurs whether or not the mother is absent because of her work, but is often especially difficult for the woman to cope with if she was out of contact because of work commitments.

I have often discussed these anxieties with women away from their children at conferences, who describe feeling raised levels of anxiety whenever they hear a phone ringing in the distance. A few years of experience of young children has raised their anxiety levels to such a pitch. I think there is also a physiological reaction to being any distance away from your children and that the distance of separation that is easily bearable changes as the children grow older and the mother becomes more experienced at being away. Many women report physical sensations of nausea, abdominal pain and headache at leaving young children, particularly for the first time in a new situation or with a new carer. Such symptoms tend to disappear rapidly if a mother is aware of what is causing them. Babies and children also may demonstrate their initial anxieties about their mother's absence, but as long as the replacement is kind and appropriate for them their anxieties are also usually short-lived. Mothers need to give clear messages about when they are going and when they are coming back as soon as their child is old enough to understand the message. Again knowledge is a safeguard against anxiety.

It is difficult to know how many of these responses to separation from her child in a working mother are 'natural' physiological responses and how much they are encouraged by society. Undoubtedly women who have a number of friends with children, who are themselves going out to work, seem to suffer less from the stress, anxiety and guilt than those who are breaking new ground among their social circle. Our mental well-being is often a reflection of how comfortable we are within a circle of friends, acquaintances and colleagues, and if our model of life differs greatly from theirs it increases our own sense of personal unease. Most of us are not so sure of ourselves as adults, and especially as parents, that we are able to totally dismiss criticisms from those around us, particularly if they appear to be united in their view and we alone are at odds with them.

Societies go through phases of wanting their mothers to be at home with their children, and find many ways of pressurising the women into whatever is deemed socially desirable. If, however, the situation demands it, during wartime, for example, mothers will be called to work outside their homes, and the importance of full-time mothering is then no longer given any prominence. Men are as influenced by the whims of society and the needs of the day as are women. They may be sent to die in countries they have never before heard of or asked to do things, and play parts which they despise, in the name of duty or obligation. It is most painful, however, for a mother to realise that much of the special relationship she has had with her children is also heavily contaminated by what her society demanded of her at the time. To go against the stream of society then is costly in terms of feeling at odds with your peers and unsupported and criticised by everyone. To go along with the dictates of society may also eventually be a disillusioning experience. Parenting is a very grown-up business. The style in which you undertake it has to feel right for you. Pleasing or appeasing others is not a long-term alternative to making up your own mind.

The relationship with her husband, boyfriend, or father of the baby will also impact upon the paid working woman for better or worse. Although I shall look at this relationship in more detail in Chapter 7 it is important to underline several elements in the context of this discussion. Many couples are drawn from the same profession or occupation because they have met during training. If they are also the same age they will be at similar points in their careers when their children are born. Most careers are competitive and that sense of competition between peers can extend to partners. I have seen a number of couples who use parenthood in some way in the course of that competition. Most commonly the father uses the fact of his partner's conversion to motherhood to suggest that she should work part-time, in a less career-orientated position than his own. Couples whose jobs have made it necessary to live in different towns, and who commute in order to be with one another, tend to move back together once a child is born. Almost always it is the woman who moves and it is the resulting upheaval, rather than motherhood itself, which has a serious effect on her future career.

A man who has been able to accept his woman as a colleague and partner in a working life may find that he cannot demonstrate the same acceptance to the mother of his children. There are many ways in which men contrive to make the paid working woman's life harder at home. I have seen couples where the man is more difficult and argumentative as soon as she goes back to work, to such an extent that these women often make several failed attempts to return to work. These situations are often compounded by the fact that the woman is ambivalent about continuing her job anyway and therefore vulnerable to pressures from her partner. Many jobs involve rejection, failed competition, repeated attempts to pass exams or make the grade. If the woman is being repeatedly undermined at home, and at the same time is attempting to cope with those pressures at work, it is no wonder that she feels something has to give. Very few working women get the same level of support from their male partners, both emotional and practical, that men expect from them. Therefore most of these women are setting off to work each day without the same sense of back-up at home. For most of us home is the safe haven we seek at the end of the day, when we are tired, stressed and feeling rejected or uncared for. The vast majority of women who go out to work will say they are constructing and maintaining this haven more or less single-handedly as well as working. By failing to meet the challenge of sharing that burden many men express their anger passively.

It is noticeable that successful women are often either single or married to men much older than themselves, men who have surmounted the competitive phase of their own careers before fatherhood and can therefore psychologically afford to be more supportive to the woman they live with. Even women who work at non-competitive, non-career jobs report that their husbands feel threatened by their gains of financial freedom and opportunities to talk to other men and women.

When women return to work after taking maternity leave they find a variety of responses awaiting them. For some there will be great relief expressed at having them back, coupled with a hope that 'now things can get back to normal'. This denies that a major change has happened in the life of that woman. How we function at work is undoubtedly changed by parenthood. I think it improves most people but at times at the cost of not giving their total attention and commitment to work. Many occupations are wary of the returning mother for this reason. I know that in medicine there is a fear that if too many mothers with small children come back to full-time work, standards of patient care will deteriorate. Hence mothers are usually persuaded back to part-time jobs, partly by being made to feel guilty about leaving their babies for long duty hours and partly by the insinuation that the care they will be able to provide to patients will be less consistent and threatened with interruptions. I have never seen any proof that either fear is justified: on the contrary, part-time work is often in reality full-time work with half the recognition and half the pay! However, I have long been aware that my male colleagues use their jobs as excuses for their lack of parenting, their late nights away from the family and their lack of availability for everything, from disasters at home to school plays. To have a female colleague doing the same job, as well as being an adequate parent, exposes these excuses for what they are, not necessarily to the men involved who are naturally reluctant to grasp the point but certainly to their partners. Some of the consultants I worked for when I was training have undoubtedly seen more of my children than their own! Paid working women need to be aware of this dynamic because many of the professional institutions are organised in such a way as to give the men involved the ultimate in excuses for avoiding parental responsibility. Women who do the same job just as well without also using it as an excuse represent a considerable threat to the power of those institutions.

Many men also envy women having time off for maternity leave. It is hard for them to welcome back colleagues without expressing that envy in some way. Envy is the most destructive of emotions and can blight what was previously an extremely good relationship without the woman being aware of much change initially. She may feel relief, as well as the mixed negative emotions discussed earlier in the chapter, to be back at work. She may feel ambivalent about motherhood and eager to get back to having adult-to-adult communications with her colleagues. It can come as an unpleasant surprise that at least initially some of those colleagues may be decidedly frosty towards her. Like many of the reactions towards mothers with young children the intensity dies down as the child becomes older. One female colleague advised me to be patient when I complained about problems of male envy at childbirth and child/mother intimacy. 'Once they think you're menopausal, you'll find they're as nice as pie again!' she said.

We have seen many of the negative emotions and responses that will face the working mother. But it is also true that women who go out to work are very much healthier in both mind and body than their stay-at-home contemporaries. This may reflect the fact that a great deal of ill-health is simply a reflection of dis-ease with our lives; working women may have the dual stress of two lives but they also enjoy the protection of having two major spheres of interest, so that if home is difficult, work is all right and vice versa. Women often feel that going out to work is a privilege and that it represents considerably less challenge and hard work than life at home, with the bonus of pay and perks. Their attitude, like that of many men, often changes during midlife, when suddenly they think of themselves working until retirement and begin to develop a distinctly more jaundiced attitude towards work. For those who truly feel they have the choice to work or not it does represent something of a luxury.

Being paid for a job carries with it a certain status. You are recognised as an important and worthwhile adult within the community in a way that women who are mothers and wives without paid work are not. Having your own money also brings with it freedom. Having your own career and being able to earn as much as most men gives you even more freedom. Choice and the freedom to choose are also important contributors to health and a sense of well-being. Women who maintain their ability to parent in this external way as well as developing the internal mothering skills often grow in confidence and become strong and capable parents. Certainly they are less dependent on the good will and good intentions of their partners and can survive better if the relationship fails. Women who go out to work tend to develop circles of their own friends who are not directly connected to their partner and/or his job. With such friends there is the possibility of greater honesty between women without any effect on their men or their men's careers.

For intelligent and educated women motherhood has never and will never be a substitute for using their gifts and their knowledge creatively and to recognised effect in the outside world. Motherhood may well enhance their abilities and increase their confidence however, and weaving motherhood together with a career can, if exhausting, also prove to be beneficial to her whole family and her community. Suddenly realising that this is the case can be an inspiration to many a woman who has laboured under the dual stress with guilt for years before enlightenment.

Many of the paid working women I know and see wish that they had had working mothers too. They have a need for models and for a sharing of experience. In this generation of women much of that experience has to be gained afresh and between peer groups. However there will be a pool of knowledge, thoughts, feelings, experiences and tales tragic and wonderful to tell our daughters and granddaughters about life as a paid working mother.

6

MEN AFTER MOTHERHOOD

A woman's transition to being a mother does not occur in a vacuum but most usually within a relationship with a man. The man is commonly although not always the father of the child. This arrangement with its legal boundaries laid down by marriage is held to be the proper and safe way to look after children. Society insinuates that marriage is for both the creation of children and then the protection of those children and their mothers.

Although many couples will acknowledge that they wish to have children few say that they are getting married specifically to procreate. Hence the expectations of marriage for one or both of the couple may include much that is unrelated to parenthood . . . companionship, shared adult interests, home-making or business partnership. In many ways those values which are often suggested to be of much worth in choosing a partner . . . shared work, interests, hobbies, likes and dislikes . . . may be relatively meaningless or even detrimental in choosing a co-parent. As one couple said to me, 'We might have been very close to each other when the children were conceived but since then it feels as if we have not had a moment to ourselves for years.' Hence the relationship which starts off as an exclusively one-to-one affair with much desire for time, attention and caring from the other partner has to be able to change into a triangular relationship where the third person is placing demands on both of the other two, thereby lessening what they can hope to give or gain from each other.

Prior to parenthood marriage is potentially able to meet the emotional and practical needs of the adults concerned.

Time and effort can be made on each other's behalf. There is time to do things together and time to be alone. There is space to organise life around the needs of the adults involved and time to negotiate and even argue in privacy and peace. The arrival of a baby changes that sense of time and space within the relationship dramatically. Suddenly there is a third and demanding person in the centre of the original one-to-one affair who takes up a great deal of time in an endless, unpredictable and unnegotiable way. Space, both physically within the living space and psychologically within the relationship, becomes less. Both parents may perceive that lack of psychological space and time as a form of prison. Their relationship ceases to feed them in its need to meet the demands of the baby..

For mature adults, with strong internal resources and a non-stressful present environment this sudden change away from personal satisfaction and towards personal sacrifice is challenging and fulfilling. They can relish their new-found roles and find a different form of satisfaction in sharing new stresses and burdens. For those who prepared for parenthood and who had some knowledge of the reality of caring for a small baby, those early weeks with seemingly relentless demands are no surprise. However, most of us are not very mature when we embark on parenting. Many parents lack the internal resources necessary for the long trek through childhood and many become parents in difficult and impoverished situations that provide further external stress.

Parenthood changes mothers and fathers differently and at different rates. The experience of parenthood can therefore cause sudden and unexpected rifts in a relationship. As one couple said, 'Mary seemed to have eased herself into becoming a mother from the moment she knew she was pregnant and so the birth and the early weeks were not such a great shock for her. Peter had not thought much about the baby being real and so when it arrived he was completely taken by surprise.' Mary experienced this difference as a rapid form of growing-up in herself and felt angry that Peter could not 'keep up'. 'As soon as I knew I was pregnant I began to talk to myself about responsibilities and began to think about re-arranging my life. I had begun to share my life with the baby a long time before the birth and so I had prepared a space for the baby in my mind.' Peter felt that Mary was 'suddenly different'. 'I'd married someone who was great fun. She was out-going and always there with a joke. Quite suddenly she seemed to change and not be interested in anyone else except the baby. I felt quite excluded.'

In therapy Mary and Peter had to explore the fact that Mary had begun to make psychological adaptations towards parenthood nearly a year earlier than Peter. Rather than attempt to follow her in those adaptations Peter had become preoccupied with what was changing in their relationship to his detriment. Often he would say something like, 'I wanted Mary to do something for me and she just seemed unavailable.' Rather than use the time to think about fatherhood and make earlier adjustments himself he became angry with Mary. The change in their relationship was her fault, it was she who had changed. Meanwhile Mary was angry with Peter and saw the deterioration in their relationship as his fault, it was he who had not changed when change was necessary.

This battle between changing and not changing reflects the interests of the couple. Partners who can cope with change both in and around themselves and who want to become parents take up the challenge of parenthood earlier in the process than those who fear change or who are not interested or involved with parenting. It is usually, although not always, the man who finds the adaptation hardest and is most reluctant to give up on the pleasures of one-to-one relating with the woman. This is because of a combination of pressures on both partners. The woman has the reality of pregnancy inside her constantly to remind her of the process in which she is involved. She cannot leave the foetus behind for a moment, it is part of her, body and mind, and to some extent she grows in her relationship with it as the foetus grows. The early attachment and relationship growth is the reason why many women are distressed by abortion, miscarriage and stillbirth. Although the world sees these events as the loss of a potential human being, to many women they are the loss of a person who already exists and has a relationship with her. Many men experience a form of unreality during pregnancy as if the pregnancy might go on for ever or as if the outcome will be somehow different to the production of a baby. Obviously this is a kind of denial of the enormity of change that is about to occur. Reality is not forced on them in the same insistent and unavoidable way that it is forced onto the mind of the pregnant woman and so they can, if they wish, ignore it.

Social expectation that women change with motherhood is much greater than any expectation that the father will change. There is the practical expectation that motherhood will change the basic pattern of a woman's life, an expectation that is rarely also attached to the father of the child. There is also an expectation of psychological change. Mothers are kind, giving, caring sorts of people in social mythology and so whatever the personality of the mother preconception there is an expectation that she will suddenly become a nicer person all round. Society expects men to change their behaviour after fatherhood but not necessarily their character. Therefore social expectations of change are deeper and more all-encompassing for the woman and once again allow men to avoid changing internally.

It is therefore easily possible for a couple who were at a similar point of maturity nine months earlier, with much in common, to reach delivery already far apart. The woman is prepared for the coming onslaught and has already begun the journey towards accepting responsibility of the life of another human being. She has also begun to form a relationship with that other being. The man has allowed himself to avoid or deny what was happening and is suddenly faced with a situation that surprises and frightens him. This is a testing time for both sides of the partnership. If the couple can mutually recognise what has happened things can change rapidly. After just two sessions of therapy Peter said, 'I feel as if the growing-up I should have done over several years is having to happen overnight. It is hard work but such a relief to feel that Mary and I are back doing something together.'

Sadly for many couples it is the beginning of a long and painful splitting. Despite much advice to wives to 'be aware that their husbands might feel left out' and to 'save a little of yourself to reassure him that he is still the centre of your life', the vast majority of new mothers are struggling to cope for themselves and their babies and can do without having to help another adult struggling in the same situations. Far from wanting to support their husbands they have hoped that the notion that marriage was to protect the mother/baby unit would now come into play so that they can cope with the new baby while the husband holds the world at bay. Meanwhile fathers who have failed to begin the adaptation during pregnancy not uncommonly share Peter's initial resentment that their women are changing in ways that take attention and caring away from themselves and towards the baby. In the sleepless and anxiety-prone nights of the early weeks of parenting such resentments can grow rapidly. The man rapidly regresses to an emotionally younger age in competition with the baby as a desperate attempt to regain the status quo. Peter had developed a bad back which required that he lay in bed and had to be fed by Mary within weeks of the arrival of their first child. All his symptoms of back pain disappeared abruptly when he began to understand that he had been unknowingly using them to get the degree of caring out of Mary which reassured him.

Given that support and protection of the mother/baby unit is implied as a major benefit of marriage to women it is perhaps surprising how few object strongly when they discover that their husbands do not change into strong and protective men when they become fathers. Often they comment that they had always known that they would end up with two children instead of one, acknowledging and accepting the regression of their husbands back towards immaturity. Such acceptance at the time tends to conceal the anger of the women and yet in therapy, sometime many years later, they will express great bitterness at their husbands' inability to grow up and accept the increased responsibilities and burdens in the same way as they perceive themselves as having done.

Hence it is possible for both partners to feel angry with each other and yet have difficulty expressing it or doing anything about it. This anger adds momentum to the growing apart psychologically within the relationship. For as long as we bring boys up without adequate models of how they can be caring fathers, and for as long as we continue on the one hand to imply that marriage provides a man to protect a woman and children, while at the same time acknowledging a lack of expectation that men will change and mature with fatherhood, we are building the environment in which men and women contract together to do a very difficult job without any real hope that that job will be equally shared by both partners. The contract is bogus as long as there is any loophole that allows one partner to avoid personal growth at the expense of the other.

The father's role in the early days of child-rearing is not clearly spelt out in any psychological theory. Whether a man has achieved an adult and responsible stance in parenting is not seen as an important parameter in judging his general psychological development. However, family therapists have begun to realise the importance of good fathering within families in recent years and have begun to describe the functions that fathers may hope to fulfil. Firstly there is a need to provide a barrier, practically, financially and emotionally, between the mother/baby unit and the stresses of the outer world for several months after delivery. This outer world may include other small children and senior members who can cause a great deal of stress at this time. Creating and maintaining such a barrier may require rapidly developing new skills of coping with fractious toddlers and difficult mothers-in-law, skills of dealing with and accepting adult responsibility for practical maintenance and provision of warmth, food and security – fielding any on-going problems that need mutual decisions in the short term. Most importantly it requires a negotiation between partners prior to delivery about a trusting temporary re-arrangement in sharing tasks. Many women simply do not trust their partners to cope sensibly with the day-to-day tasks of the family and household. However well based such lack of trust is in past experience lack of this form of negotiation means that the man is left without a clear role to fulfil, without goals to meet and with little clear expectation of what he should be achieving psychologically. There are few, if any, cultural parameters to tell him what to do.

Secondly, at a time that feels comfortable to both parents, the father needs to evolve a role with the new baby. The timing and extent of this varies greatly and again needs some overt negotiation; each parent may well have differing views on the subject which need to be heard and understood by the other even if they strongly disagree. However, it is the evolution of this role that allows the mother to begin another stage in her own separation from the baby, releasing her to re-engage in other relationships and occupations.

We all need mothering not just as children but also as adults when stressed or ill. We need to be able to sink back into that sensation of being cared about, at least momentarily, in order to replenish our resources. Men find it much easier to continue their demands for mothering on their partners; mothering, after all, sounds like something only women do for others. Women, and most particularly women who have just had babies, forget that they too need mothering if they are to cope with the new stresses without undue psychological pain. Many men find it hard to 'mother'. They have not been taught how to do it and fear that they may be seen as less manly if they turn out to be good at it. Hence women commonly turn to their female relatives and friends for emotional and practical support in preference to their partners. This highly practical solution for the woman leads to an even greater distancing within the parental relationship with decreasing demands being made on the man to mature and cope, coupled with increasing resentment and bitterness that he has not proved able to do these things.

Sally, a 23-year-old with one daughter aged 8 months, married to Dan, a 26-year-old builder, said, 'I didn't really expect him to do anything. My dad had never done anything with us so I just took it as normal that he continued his life as if nothing had happened whilst my life changed completely. Then after three months I began to get angry with him about anything . . . any little problem I would blame on him and go on and on about it whatever he said. Then I stopped and thought that he was no use to me at all and that I'd be better off without him.' Sally left Dan and took her daughter back to live with her parents for a while. We met in therapy as an extended family, Sally, Dan, and Sally's parents. They were all unhappy with what was happening and each member was angry with all the others. Sally clung to her daughter and shouted at Dan, who kept saying that he was confused and did not know what was happening, making her even more angry. Sally's dad, Brian, was also angry with Dan and blamed him for not looking after his daughter and granddaughter more effectively.

'I earn a good wage,' retorted Dan. 'What else am I expected to do?'

'Look after her!' yelled Brian.

'What?' exploded Sally's mum, Sue. 'You're a fine one to talk. When did you ever look after me?'

Sally burst into tears at this sign of battle between her parents. 'It all went wrong for you two,' she said, 'and now it's all going to go wrong for me.'

I encouraged Sally to move out of her chair between her parents and cross the room to sit with Dan. Without prompting he put his arm around her and said, 'You sound really desperate, love.'

There was a long silence while Sally cried and Dan held her. Brian and Sue looked increasingly uncomfortable but sat very still, not looking at each other.

Finally Brian began to speak. 'I thought that children were women's work. I loved you all and I wanted to do my best but I didn't know the first thing about children.'

Very bitterly Sue said, 'Neither did I when we had Sally but I had no choice but to find out.'

The family worked together through a painful phase of getting to know each other as parents, exchanging the difficulties of being a father or mother. At the end of the last session Dan commented, 'Well, I've got Brian as a sort of model. I just ask him what he did when the children were little and then I try to do the opposite.' They all managed a laugh at this demonstration of how far along the path of re-negotiation they had all travelled.

Babies and small children can be a great deterrent to sexual activity. If the man is feeling left out and suddenly underprivileged in his relationship with his wife he may increase his sexual demands in order to make his needs known. At the same time the woman will be feeling tired, may still have anxieties about her physical health after the delivery and will be at least partly physically absorbed with the baby, therefore needing less physical stimulation or comfort from her man. In a relationship where verbal communication is just as or more important than sexual communication this transition time, taking anything from a few weeks to several years, does not cause any great tensions or rifts. Many heterosexual relationships depend on sexual communication as the major or only channel by which the couple share time, thoughts and emotions together, however, and for these couples a time when sexual activity becomes a problem or a battle represents a considerable threat to the integrity of the relationship.

When I was a medical student studying obstetrics there was a 'joke' retold to each bunch of students along the lines of:

Q. 'When is it safe to resume intercourse after delivery?'
A. 'Gentlemen wait until after the placenta is delivered!'

Sadly this 'joke' reflects that some women deliberately extend their hospital stay after delivery to avoid their husbands' inappropriate sexual overtures. Even in these supposedly liberated times of women's sexuality there is still evidence of sexual 'ownership' by men of women in marriage. Some men see a need to re-establish that ownership as rapidly as possible after a new birth in the family. Although angry and bitter about their experiences women in such relationships may well tolerate them for a lifetime, venting their anger in endless gynaecological problems and symptoms. As one patient told me after several gynae operations ending with a hysterectomy, 'I wanted him to know how much he had damaged my insides.' She discovered that allowing a gynaecologist to take away a variety of different organs did not remove her anger and humiliation. After many months of therapy she was able to say, 'I would recommend any woman to get out sooner rather than later if she finds herself married to a man who thinks he owns her. I wish I had thought less of being a good wife and had been more judgmental about whether or not he was a good husband years ago.'

Such extremes may be decreasing but the modern-day

'yuppie' equivalent is, I think, the men who accompany their wives to all obstetric and gynae appointments and wish to discuss the details with the doctor, often interrupting any conversation that might have otherwise occurred between doctor and woman. This is a more subtle form of ownership but often leaves the woman feeling depressed without understanding why.

I met Sandra when she was 28. She and Brian, her husband, had had several years of investigation for infertility. At our first meeting she told me proudly that Brian had come to every appointment that she had ever attended. 'He's not like most men, not interested in that sort of thing. He really wants to see me sorted out,' she said.

Why then, I asked, had she phoned her GP only days after discovering that she was pregnant to say that she was so unhappy that she had contemplated killing herself?

Brian, who had insisted on coming into my room with Sandra, despite a request to sit in the waiting-room, then launched into a long monologue about his interpretation of events. He was a rational, intelligent man who presented himself as charming, frank and easy to talk to whereas Sandra spoke very softly, making it hard to hear or understand her, and sat with her head bowed making no eye contact. As Brian continued I watched Sandra withdraw even further into herself.

I pointed out to this couple what was happening in the room between the three of us. 'Brian, it is rather as if you are a parent who has brought a young child along to see me,' I suggested. 'Are you frightened about letting Sandra tell her own version of your story?'

'I'm telling you what happened,' he explained as if the notion that Sandra might see things differently was totally alien to him.

'You're telling me what happened to you,' I explained, 'and you are demonstrating this morning just how capable you are at dealing with these appointments, talking to a doctor and speaking on Sandra's behalf. Now I think it would be a good idea if we heard from Sandra, who obviously finds the situation much more difficult to cope with.'

During the next hour, as Sandra's story was told, I had to

make repeated attempts to silence Brian, even threatening to make him leave the room if he could not be quiet. He and Sandra saw his interruptions as attempts to 'rescue' and 'look after' her initially, but as the hour wore on and her story told of her bitterness at the lack of communication between herself and the obstetrician, her exclusion from the decision-making process of how to continue investigations, and their final meeting when the pregnancy was confirmed, when Brian and the obstetrician had shaken hands and congratulated each other, totally ignoring Sandra, it became clear that Brian's ease of communication had hindered the quieter Sandra from any chance of adequate communication.

'Maybe she can talk to you because you are a woman,' Brian commented.

'I certainly felt as if you and the obstetrician were part of an all-male club,' said Sandra. 'You both made me feel as if you'd conceived our child together like a couple of surrogate parents and this baby inside me is nothing to do with me.'

Obviously Brian would not have been able to take over in the way he had without Sandra backing down and allowing him to do so. However, many women observe that their husbands find it easier to talk to male doctors and take over in similar ways in such conversations. I had felt as if I might have to gag Brian or remove him from the room in order to get enough space for Sandra to begin to talk, and she did not have the personal energy to achieve that for herself. Happily there was much room for change in this relationship and by the time that Clare arrived, six months later, Sandra had learnt a great deal about asserting herself and Brian had begun to learn to listen as well as speak.

Even within a more balanced and equal relationship the issue of who 'owns' the woman's body can cause problems. Undoubtedly the baby considers that it has first call on mum's body and meeting those expectations may be as much or more than a woman can cope with in terms of physical demands. A partner suggesting intimacy or attempting seduction, however kind and insightful, may be perceived as yet another demand to fulfil another person's need rather than her own. Undoubtedly the women who are allowed the space to emerge from the physical closeness of the first six to twelve weeks of motherhood probably return to sexual activities with more enthusiasm. There is a need for time and space to recapture the sense of having your body to yourself again and a need to know that the boundaries, physical and emotional, are healed before intimacy feels safe. For many women this process takes months. The more difficult the delivery, the more demanding the baby and the more persistent the man on his own behalf, the less likely that the woman will feel excited or will gain satisfaction, reassurance and comfort from sexual experiences. After such a major loss of control as pregnancy, delivery, breast-feeding and the early days of mothering, further losses in terms of excitement and orgasm often come to seem horrendous rather than happy. Most women can sense when they are ready to 'let go' of themselves again and there is no good reason why they should feel any pressure from any direction to do so before feeling ready. Impatience with the natural process of healing and restoration can only lead to long-term bitterness and damage.

At the other end of the spectrum lies an unconscious belief which many adults share and that is that parents are not sexual beings. It is, of course, a paradoxical belief, as we are all the results of sexual activity between our parents and yet for most of us imaging that sexual activity is very difficult. For some couples this unconscious belief rears its head in their own sexual relationship once they become parents. Such couples are apt to call each other 'mummy' and 'daddy', giving priority in their relationship to those roles to the exclusion of other ones. It is not that such couples necessarily cease to have sexual intercourse but rather that they lose the young enthusiastic approach and develop a rather grim and dutiful alternative that gradually erodes each of them. Sex becomes a function of what must be done, like housework or car maintenance, with little pleasure and little communication. It is not uncommon to hear from couples separating once the children leave home that sex ceased to be enjoyable once they became parents and that they never regained their initial happiness physically. Couples only tend to ask for help if one or other of them believes that they should be enjoying sex despite being parents. Often a simple understanding of why it is difficult to be sexy parents, for instance, if that is not the model given to you by your own parents or if you are envious of the parent of your own sex having intimate and loving times with your other parent, helps to broaden the sense of freedom of choice in sexuality again.

Children are naturally sexually curious and will want to see what their parents do together if given half a chance. Many parents find that a powerful inhibitory force. Like so much in parenthood it is the coming to terms with our own difficulties and restrictions that frees us to give as much as we would like to our children.

The model of relationships provided by parents during the child's early life form a template of expectations of future relationships for that child. It is in the sorting out of the difficulties, airing problems and working through them realistically together, that the child grows to know that relationships are dynamic and fluid affairs in which you have rights as well as duties. The men who bemoan what they have lost and seek to recapture it by regressing into childhood themselves miss the fundamental point of and challenge in parenting. The women who seek to protect their men from the realities of child-rearing in order to 'keep the peace' are also providing a distorted model of what healthy relating is all about. The men who run from reality and responsibility and the women who collude with them help nobody in the end, least of all the baby.

7

MOTHERING ALONE

A large number of women spend at least part of their time as mothers coping alone. This is not only true for separated and divorced women, although they are the largest group that spring to mind when single-parent families are mentioned. There is also a large but hidden group of women who parent alone inside of marriage, women married to sailors, for instance. Many women relate a sense of mothering alone even within conventional marriages when the husband is not usually absent. Many of the women I have had the opportunity to talk to over the years say that when they do eventually become acknowledged as single parents, after divorce or when their husbands go away on prolonged business trips, they suddenly realise that they are not doing any more than previously and that in many ways coping alone with children has many advantages. Few women choose to parent alone however. Most become mothers in the belief that it is something they are going to do with their partners and therefore the discovery that this is not in fact the case will be tinged with bitterness and disillusionment.

Becoming a single parent is usually a traumatic process with much heated and confused emotion in the relationships over and above the basic problem of having to cope with small children as just one adult figure. Divorce, death, and dealing with new partners and their children, all add to the picture of parenting chaos inherent in such transitions. In the early days of being alone most women find that it is within their network of female friends that salvation lies. Not only does this provide a source of adult support, conversation and humour, it also provides hope of practical help and advice. Undoubtedly single parents have become a force to be reckoned with since these small groups banded together into national bodies to represent their interests. The children also benefit from mixing with other children who may have already gone through the process of losing a parent and surviving. Children often feel hostile towards the remaining parent, sensing that in some way they are responsible for the absence of the missing parent. In many cases this is cruel and unjust, but the woman left behind to cope needs to understand that the child is trying desperately to make sense of the confusion of the situation. Making mother responsible for the chaos and unhappiness is one way of the child feeling that someone powerful is still in control. Statements from children at this time can be remarkably painful and provocative. Children may also regress back to an earlier time of development, at least for a while, as a means of expressing their unhappiness. This all puts much added strain onto a woman who is very probably trying hard to keep life as normal as possible for the children, while her own life feels painful, vulnerable and chaotic.

Often there are serious practical considerations to becoming a single parent. Housing may need to change, finances are almost always restricted, and the woman may need to seek work, perhaps for the first time in years. It is this scenario that should be firmly expressed to the idealistic 18-year-olds who, with all the chances of training, careers and being able to protect their incomes and status for themselves and their children if they should end up alone, still choose to see a marriage as a woman's salvation. All the statistics suggest they are wrong and we are failing in our education of future generations unless that is pointed out to them. Women left alone with children are not usually well off, indeed they are one of the poorest groups of adults in the country. The poverty tends to have a grinding effect on the woman, who may cope well for months or years with hardship and then suddenly find herself physically and emotionally drained, feeling she cannot go on any more. It is for this reason that most recent advice to women who are left alone with children centres around plans for training and future work. Going back to some form of training full- or part-time in the immediate aftermath of becoming a single parent often offers the woman a chance to catch up on parts of growing up that she has missed, while at the same time requiring hours and commitments more likely to fit in with parenthood than most work. In the longer term it is always to her advantage to plan a working life and to move towards financial independence and less poverty. The vast majority of women have not been educated to their full potential and therefore there is almost always room for improving their qualifications. It allows the woman to take a positive attitude towards herself and her future, something which many women alone with small children find hard to do.

A number of studies following up the fortunes of single-parent mothers have concluded that it is the quality of the interpersonal relationships, particularly with other women, that make the difference to coping or not during the first five years. After that, although women still rate friendship as an important factor in their sanity they rate having gained further education and holding down a job they enjoy as most important in their satisfaction.

Education or work both allow the woman access to other adults without the continuous presence of the children. Being solely responsible for a number of young lives is a wearing obligation and, however much loved and wanted the children, most women feel they need to get away regularly in order to maintain that level of responsible caring. Although working outside the home increases practical pressures in her life, it also means that she has other places where she can vent her feelings. Many mothers who are alone with children find themselves becoming depressed because there is nowhere and no one with whom they can let rip with their angry and frustrated feelings. They are often sadly aware of how much the children have already been exposed to arguments, fights and abuse during relationship breakdowns and want to keep the peace now that they are alone with them. They do this at considerable cost to themselves, however. Other women will report feeling dismayed and guilty because of how much they find themselves shouting at the children. I suspect that mothers alone often become hypersensitive to their own mothering, being critical about the human lapses in parenting that most parents take for granted. If you are with another adult it does not matter too much if the mother is totally unreasonable for a day or so just because she is tired and unwell or stressed. If that mother is the only caring adult in the family her unreasonableness may seem more frightening to the children and more destructive and reprehensible to herself.

It is reported that there is more violence amongst single-parent families towards children, although this is a difficult statistic to evaluate as many single parents are living with or seeing a lot of at least one other adult figure who may be a major source of violence. However, the strains of parenthood, undiluted and unshared, are burdensome indeed and undoubtedly some mothers do become increasingly violent in response to what they see as an impossible load. Often women who are lonely and unsupported feel trapped into a vicious spiral of caring for others but getting nothing back for themselves, which rapidly depletes their abilities to cope with the frustrations of motherhood in any other way except lashing out.

It represents a major emotional problem to be both the sole source of love and comfort and the soul source of discipline. To combine both of these elements of parenting requires an ability to slip from one to the other rapidly, but equally to be able to forgive, forget and slide back again. This sort of shifting in relationships requires a sense of self, a notion of what is just and reasonable within that self and an acceptance that loving relationships contain hate and despair as well as love and comfort. In the long term children brought up with one or more adults who are able to encompass both aspects of parenting fluently probably have more realistic ideas on relationships than those brought up in houses where parental functions are still rigidly stereotyped. Most single mothers have not been brought up this way, however, and are therefore breaking new psychological ground. Many women came into therapy with guilty admissions that they do not seem to be able to be both parents. It is important to realise that no one adult can be two people . . . a mother alone with her son for instance cannot try to spell out what both mummy and daddy would say in any situation . . . but what is required is that the essential elements of parenting which are love and boundaries, caring and discipline, are embodied within the one parent.

The feelings that the woman continues to have for the father of the child can colour the relationship she manages to form. If there are several children one is almost certain to be like the father, to have the looks or the mannerisms which she remembers, either fondly or with disgust. As the children grow into teenagers these resemblances can become even more marked. Some women attempt to compensate for this by ignoring or even punishing all that is like the father in the child. Other women, particularly those who have been widowed, may attempt to keep special much-loved characteristics of the lost husband alive in one or all of the children. Any of these ploys for temporary relief emotionally for the mother tend to have long-term detrimental effects on all concerned. The children grow up confused between what they think they are meant to be and who they actually are; the mother fails to fully grieve the lost husband and, instead of allowing him to emotionally die from her life over a period of years, he is kept alive in her relationship with the children, making it difficult for them eventually to grow away from her. Similarly, a mother who has been deserted may, in anger, wish to annihilate features of that husband from the child as an alternative to doing the emotional work on herself, which is necessary to put the relationship and his rejection of herself into focus with the remainder of her life.

Many women are initially overwhelmed by the emotions leading up to the aloneness as parents, and fall, in crisis, into patterns of relating to the children which make their suffering marginally more bearable. As with most crisis solutions to life's distress this is a short-term answer and is only healthy in the short term.

The majority of women alone with children, despite poverty and many practical and emotional difficulties, seem to cope remarkably well. I have rarely heard a woman who has coped alone for a few years expressing any great desire to return to shared parenting. Most find that working through the difficulties, learning to be a single source of both loving and disciplining, and building a new life outside the home to strengthen their financial and emotional ability to function within the home adds considerably to their self-esteem and confidence. Many say that after several years they feel 'like new women'. Often I hear expressions like 'I hardly recognise myself now as the wife and mother I started out as.' Certainly there are privileges as well as perils in the situation. As one mum said to me, 'I run a benign dictatorship and with three small children it works a great deal better than our earlier attempts at marital democracy.' Decisions can be made in the full knowledge that there is no other adult to question them, plans into the future can be plotted without fear that someone else's job will interrupt with them, and friendships can be formed and allowed to mature without the distorting effect of an always present partner. These benefits undoubtedly add strength to a mother in the eyes of her children. She is no longer a martyr to dad, no longer beaten or abused in front of them, not humiliated or ridiculed if she speaks her mind, and now, when she says what she means, she has the freedom to mean what she says. These are by no means small perks to compensate for the rigours of life alone with children. I know of no good research to suggest that children brought up by mothers who take advantage of these perks and cope with the difficulties are in any way more psychologically damaged than children brought up in the supposedly 'normal' nuclear family. In the losing of one parent, the child may well be losing two inadequate parents who undermined each other and getting one much more capable one in exchange. It is not perfect . . . but then what in parenting is?

8

MOTHERS, DAUGHTERS, GRANDMOTHERS AND OTHER WOMEN

A woman's primary relationship is with her mother. For many women the first relationship remains the most central and intense of all their relationships. Despite its importance it is often ignored in the theoretical assumptions about the development of a woman's personality, with lip-service paid to crucial good early mothering but more interest shown in the supposed leap of attachment made from mother towards father between the ages of 3 and 5. This is considered to be the normal healthy developmental path for small girls, although why a small child should 'give up on' the primary parent who cares, feeds, cuddles and protects her and invest all her future hopes in a much more distant father-figure is never clearly explained. Theory assumes it is a leap towards attachment with the father but in my experience with women in therapy it seems much more likely that, if and when such a leap does occur, it is as much a leap away from the mother as a leap towards intimacy with father; away from the disillusionment suffered in the relationship with mother and towards a dream, a hope of goodness and proper caring.

The mother/daughter relationship is a heated, ambivalent and competitive relationship. Ann Oakley discovered while interviewing new mothers in London in the mid-1970s that a staggering 44 per cent of mothers would admit to being disappointed in the birth of a daughter. Only 8 per cent claimed disappointment with a son. From the beginning therefore nearly half the mother/daughter relationships start with a sense of reserve on behalf of the mothers . . . a sense of reserve which has nothing to do with their new daughters' personalities but to do with them simply being female. It is alarming how many women spend the rest of their lives trying to be good enough to overcome that primary sense of disappointment in their mothers, getting increasingly frustrated and depressed when whatever they do, however hard they try, all their endeavours end in failure. Knowing that mother's disappointment started a long while before she 'knew' the daughter as a person sometimes helps to make sense of the despair women feel about these relationships.

Why should women feel sad to have a daughter though? Susie Orbach and Louise Eichenbaum, writing about their experiences with women in therapy, suggest two reasons for this source of sadness. Firstly daughters are more likely to stir up uncomfortable feelings in the mother. A helpless and vulnerable son may make a woman feel strong and capable with a dependent male figure for the first time in her life, while a helpless new baby girl reminds the mother that she was once helpless and vulnerable . . . feelings she may have fought hard against and be unwilling to re-examine. Her life may feel too fragile, dependent and vulnerable as an adult to bear any thought about similar feelings as a child. The more ambivalent or neglectful her own care as a baby the greater the pain of watching the helpless new daughter. One way to deal with that pain is to distance the daughter's neediness, either by denial or by repeating the pattern of neglect. Women will often confirm that they treat their daughters differently to their sons but will explain these differences in terms of the children's different needs. Daughters are perceived as needing less, and from a very early age are felt to be more emotionally independent.

An American psychologist attempted to explore these different perceptions of need by dressing the same baby first as a girl and then as a boy and presenting it to the same group of women whose behaviour was videoed. Differences in behaviour were readily apparent on the video, and each woman when questioned managed to find an explanation in terms of the baby's behaviour, rather than her own expectations, for her different reactions. The baby behaved differently on the two occasions as a result of the differing behaviour it received from the women. As a boy it was continually held, talked to and played with. After a brief period of this behaviour the baby became more demanding of further stimuli. As a girl the baby was placed on the floor 'to crawl' or even into the cot 'to rest', and soon ceased to demonstrate the demanding behaviour it had learnt so rapidly as a 'boy'. In this way the mother's preconceptions of what her daughter should be like, including the belief that her arrival is basically disappointing, colours her perceptions of what the daughter is like. The rapid change in the baby's behaviour shows that even small children quickly learn to understand what they can expect in any situation and behave in ways that then re-confirm the mother's original preconceptions.

The second reason suggested by Orbach and Eisenbaum for a mother's sense of disappointment and need to restrict her daughter's demands comes from her knowledge of the role she plays as a woman and the role that will be expected of her daughter by society. She knows by her own experience that acceptable female behaviour lies between narrow limits. If you spoil a daughter too much, so the myth goes, then she will not grow up into a capable carer of others. Many mothers also harbour secret hopes that their daughters will mother them. If they have had to play the little mother to their own mothers for many years it is easy to see how this expectation of role reversal may grow unchallenged. Many daughters slide into the role of carer to the mother, seeing her as helpless and vulnerable, innocent or weak. They become their mother's major confidante from an early age when they have intuitive rather than intellectual capacities for understanding another person's needs. Often they can understand her needs more fluently than any adult, which makes the daughter too precious for the mother to relinquish into further relationships either with father or subsequent girlfriends. Later on it is these mothers who are so competitive with boyfriends and son-in-laws who have 'stolen' their closest companion. Such dependence on a daughter is always tinged with anger and ambivalence, however, the mother being unable to tolerate any outward acknowledgment of just how dependent she is.

There is third reason for mother/daughter hostility and ambivalence which is based in a sense of competition. In psychological theories we hear a great deal about the child's sense of competition with the parent of the same sex and tend to dismiss the obvious fact that many parents are jealous of and competitive with children of the same sex. For the many women who see other women as 'the enemy', daughters represent the closest and most threatening part of that opposition. They are prime contenders for their fathers' feelings, and they are also younger, and often more advantaged versions of mother. The mother will be torn between wanting her daughter to be a good reflection of herself and her mothering and the sense of envy of the daughter's new life with all its hopes and dreams. The less fulfilled and more frustrated and trapped the woman, the more intense the resentment. Many successful women describe the ambivalence in their mothers towards their careers. Marsha, a 35-year-old senior nurse, said, 'My mother pushed me to succeed all through childhood, although whenever I was successful there was never a celebration. Intead my mother would detail what she had given me to make the success possible. Any failures were mine but all my successes I owed to her. When I became really successful she dismissed having a career as a worthless thing and said she had never missed it herself. She told me that I had already failed because I did not have a husband or a family. She is only really proud of me when what I do reflects on her. She can't appreciate a separate me at all.'

The more insecure a woman feels about her femininity the more likely she is to compete with her daughter. Often the mothers who push their daughters towards careers do so partly in the knowledge that they wish they had had the chance and partly in the hope that it will take their daughters' attention away from growing up into women.

Many mothers feel uncomfortable with their own sexuality, never masturbate, and feel there is something distasteful about their genitals. Each time such a mother sees her daughter naked she experiences a sense of disgust, which transmits itself to the child, laying down the foundation of her daughter's disgust with her own sexuality.

The daughter conceving and giving birth shows that she is sexually active, a fully-grown woman, who is moving on in her relationships to a new phase. It takes a mature mother to allow her daughter space at this time to create her own form of mothering. A daughter who chooses to mother in a different way to her own mother may well be seen as being critical. A mother will also want to be close to her daughter and share experiences as her daughter's pregnancy revives memories of herself at that time. This often poses difficulties for both the daughter and for her man. The mother's desire to be close may feel like an intrusion to the couple. With mothers who the daughters perceive as dangerously competitive there is always the possibility that they will attempt to steal the child away emotionally. Daughters are often torn between trusting their mothers most with the new baby as far as the baby's safety is concerned, and therefore needing the mother as a practical back-up if ill or tired, but mistrusting their mothers most in terms of the competition to be the best mum to the new baby. Grandmothers who feel they have failed their own children at some stage or who did not have all the children they wanted are most prone to this form of competition.

Against all that is negative and powerfully detrimental to the women involved, there is also much that is positive in the mother/daughter relationship and the moment they transform from mother/daughter to grandmother/mother/daughter is often the moment when the goodness, understanding, love and closeness can come to the surface. However the daughter has perceived her mother in the past, a new breeze of reality sweeps through her assessment when she becomes a mother too. She begins to understand much that has previously hurt and confused her, and, perhaps most important of all, she begins to know that mothers are only ordinary people. As one woman said to her own mother in family therapy marking this reassessment, 'Mothers are normal, doing their best in a difficult job. They're just like you and me . . . in fact they are you and me!'

The process of reassessment does not occur overnight but usually takes several years to complete. Nowadays many daughters live far away from their mothers during this transition, and miss out on the changes that can occur in the relationship in this phase, which is to everyone's disadvantage. Such young mothers often set themselves impossibly high standards of mothering because they want to be better mothers than their own mothers were to them. Allowing themselves to sometimes fail their children means forgiving their mothers for sometimes failing them. A grandmother on the end of a phone can be a great deal more threatening with advice and criticism than the granny who spends time with her young grandchildren and reminds herself just how annoying and tiring small babies are before leaping in with the unhelpful super-mum kind of advice.

Of course the capacity for change in this relationship requires that both participants have room for psychological manoeuvre. Their past experiences of each other, their relationships with the principal men in the family and other interests and sources of fulfilment outside of mothering will all colour just how far and how fast reassessment can progress. As the relationship between mother and daughter changes so does the relationship both women make with their other women friends. Young motherhood is often a time of 'discovering' female friendship and learning to value its emotional and practical support. To gain fully in such relationships any sense of competition needs to be laid aside. This can be difficult as women are encouraged to be competitive as mothers by the media and advertising as well as upbringing. Hence it is easy to become locked into the 'who has the whitest nappies in the road?' which may be helpful to the soap powder manufacturers but does little for the women involved except distance them at a time when closeness would be beneficial.

For the women who cannot achieve reassessment with mother there is always the possibility of establishing different and more close, trusting relationships with other women. The interdependence of women during mothering was an important social fact in the extended family. Even now, in cultures that still have several generations living together, questions such as 'Who will babysit?' are unknown, because a caring and involved adult (usually a woman) is always around to take care of the children. Children, even when they are very young, can be allowed more immediate freedom to explore their environment because of the much higher adult/baby ratio in the home. In Western culture all too often there is a home, one woman, several small children and not enough female interdependence to share the heavy burden. The concept of the nuclear family separates women, often leaving them alone with more child-care than one adult could reasonably be expected to cope. Female friendship and support can be viewed as a threat to the conventional set-up and actively discouraged by the male members of the family. Many women describe having to fit in their shared child-caring or socialising together into the hours their partners are at work, and immediately 'drop' that social constellation to return to the nuclear image when they come home.

One woman described it to me as, 'I feel like two people. In the daytime I get together with several other mums. We're quite a group really and we have a lot of laughs together. It really helps and supports us. Then we all scatter back to our little boxes ready for the men to come home. Then I feel much older, much less full of laughter. Then I do the things I have to do. I love my husband and want to spend time with him and yet somehow his expectations of me as wife and mother seems to hold us back from really having fun like we used to. He thinks I've changed but really as far as he is concerned I've just gone underground!'

Many women comment that they are surprised by the sense of fun and freedom they find in other women's company. Learning to re-evaluate other women leads them to re-evaluate themselves too. That re-evaluation can be very important for the mothers who have had daughters. Their early disappointment at it having been a girl may suddenly be swept away as they begin to join the women and feel increasingly confident and good about being one of them. Daughters who have difficulty with their own mothers often do experience difficulty relating to their daughters too. Patterns that they have found hurtful get passed on, however hard a woman may consciously try to be different.

Pauline was 43 when she came asking for help in her relationship to her daughter Susannah who was 17. Pauline was a rounded and warm woman with a trouble-worn face. I realised by our third session that her entire wardrobe was in tones of brown or black and there was never a hint of colour about her. Susannah, as described by her mother, was a slender and attractive girl who was meant to be studying for her 'A' levels when she found time in between her hectic social life. In many ways it became clear from this description that Susannah had all the colour and Pauline was left with a sense of boredom, duty and predictability. Unsolicited she said that she had exactly the same relationship with her mother who was also a colourful woman. 'I never felt I could compete with her,' Pauline explained, 'and so I learnt to become a backcloth for her instead. I feel that I have just gone on doing that for Susannah.' Pauline's husband, Geoff, had left her eight years earlier to live with another woman and Susannah blamed Pauline for this loss of her dad. 'If you weren't so boring,' she would say to her mother whenever Pauline was trying to discipline her, 'then dad might have stayed.'

As Pauline traced the roots of her lack of confidence to compete back to feeling very scared by her exotic mother she became increasingly sad. She realised how much of her life had been restricted by her inability to risk competition. She had never tried for promotion at her job in a bank as this involved competitive interviewing. She had made no move to win back Geoff's affections, indeed quite the reverse in that she said, 'I felt like the sort of woman a man would want to leave.' Working through her sadness she became increasingly angry at a mother who was suddenly seen as uncaring and selfish. 'I would like to get something right,' she began to say, 'just to show that old bag that I was worth much more than she gave me.' As Pauline began to develop, her relationship with Susannah began to change too. They had gone shopping for an outfit that Pauline could wear to an interview and Susannah had managed to be both helpful and diplomatic. 'She is really a very kind girl,' Pauline commented afterwards, as if surprised to find warmth for herself in their relationship. Perhaps helped by a beautiful light green suit which she wore proudly to therapy one day, Pauline gained her promotion. She said with radiant happiness, 'My mother doesn't appreciate what I've just achieved but Susannah said she was really proud of me. She says she likes having a mum she can look up to at long last.'

Certainly the most common complaint that women make about their mothers in therapy is not that they were particularly uncaring but that they were weak. The mothers who do not stand their own ground make frightening models for their daughters. The mothers who model forms of martydom do not inspire daughters. And mothers who were victims of their own mothers who then go on to let their daughters make victims out of them too often end up frightening the daughters much more than they realise. Children want to find limits, rules and strength in the parents they depend on. Most children experience their peak dependence in their relationship with their mothers and it is a truly horrifying experience to realise that the one on whom you have totally depended is too weak to even defend themselves. Such strength to be self-determining is particularly important as a model to the daughter who needs to find respect for her mother as a prerequisite to finding self-respect.

Mothers of sons have no less need of strength. In order to achieve masculinity boys have to separate psychologically from their mothers and mothers need to feel emotionally strong enough to let them go. Masculinity is defined by comparison to what is experienced from mother. Boys go through the sadness of realising that they can never be like their mothers and will never have the power of giving birth. Boys of 3 or 4 often pretend they have babies in their tummies, with pillows stuffed up their T-shirts, or become interested in mother's underwear as a desperate attempt to ward off the knowledge that they cannot be like her. Much of the outside world is unknown to them and that which they are exposed to, such as TV, tends to have a fantasy flavour that they realise does not match up with what they have seen in their fathers. Hence the way they begin to define how they are different to mother is to become opposite to her and to refuse to do the things that she does. For many women this time of drawing away is painful. They have experienced the longed-for relationship with a dependent male over whom they have had power. It is at this time that a mother tends to feel her own strength and release her son from any emotional obligation to provide that strength for her. We are all a complex mixture of male and female characteristics. The merged mother/son relationship sometimes splits those qualities so that mother invests all her more masculine qualities in the son while robbing him of his female characteristics. Health and happiness for both participants requires that that split is healed before separation.

Obviously motherhood creates different emotional experiences for the mother depending on the sex of her child and her own view, gained mostly from the mother and only secondarily from the father, of her own sexuality. If the leap towards an intimacy with dad is made primarily in order to escape a claustrophobic or hostile relationship with mum, there will be many emotions left over from that primary relationship that emerge as the woman becomes a mother herself. Fathers are often distant figures about whom it is possible to maintain more illusions. If daughters grow up to work and live in a different setting to their fathers it is possible for that idealised image of him to live on well into their adulthood. Needless to say all real men will fail that image and so she will be disillusioned by heterosexual relationships and yet, having abandoned mum to pin her hopes on dad from an early age, relationships with women may also present problems to her. Such women tend to become lonely and isolated in the early days of mothering, feeling that everything and everyone has failed them.

For all that it is probably the most difficult of relationships for many women it remains the centre of their understanding about themselves. Therefore there is no running away from sorting out the mother/daughter interaction, not by running into daddy's arms aged 5 or a husband's arms twenty years later. Understanding self, through an understanding of that primary attachment, can soothe the pain, enhance the shared and special experiences and lead the way to a more generally supportive and emotionally sustaining circle of women friends.

9

THE DEVASTATING EFFECTS OF MOTHERHOOD

One of the questions I hear young mothers asking most frequently is 'Why didn't someone tell me it would be like this?' They are referring to their sense of desolation and annihilation after the birth of their baby. It is a fascinating part of our cultural mythology that motherhood is given such a rosy write-up everywhere and that the other, much blacker, side of the bargain is hardly mentioned. This silence probably reflects the extent to which our cultural mythology is a male mythology. Women, even when they know that such mythology is wrong, tend to keep their peace rather than attempt to speak out against it. This is particulary true of the myths of motherhood when to speak against the myths risks the individual woman being branded a bad mother, a fate most women would do much to avoid. Even amongst women there is a degree of silence about the reality of mothering, each woman believing that she is somehow at fault rather than blaming a society that fails to value motherhood and make it an easier and more enjoyable process.

The sensations of anxiety and depression that are commonplace reactions to motherhood are translated by each woman in her own unique style. Hence some become listless and tearful, others become hyperactive; some allow the house, child, and self to fall to pieces around them, while others frantically clean everything and become obsessed with thoughts of germs and infections harming the baby; some talk of suicide or of harming the baby, others talk of a new-found certainty that they have a fatal illness; and a few lose the boundaries between reality and fantasy and become psychotic. All women translate the problem to fit in with their earlier patterns of coping or not coping under stress, but for many there is a single underlying problem.

Having a baby changes everything, both within and around a woman. Nothing is the same again and that overwhelming unfamiliarity is frightening to even the most capable and supported of people. Most women have children a long time before they have reached emotional maturity themselves; in fact the having of children is for many women part of that maturing process and so by definition most of us are psychologically unready for motherhood until after the event. Maternal instinct does not arrive by magic to coincide with the first birth. Either you are already familiar with babies or you have to wait until familiarity emerges over the early months. However, what often does arrive with the birth is a sense that the mother should respond to every need or whim of the baby. This reaction may be the distant echoes of the experiences of our foremothers who gave birth to children in much more dangerous times and therefore might have needed a certain amount of inbuilt martyrdom in order that the species survives. Like many of our cultural memories these instincts towards martyrdom are not only out-dated but also a handicap nowadays.

Babies are born with determination to survive. For the first few years their thoughts centre around themselves in an attempt to ensure that survival. They may look small and defenceless but they are, from their earliest days, capable of a surprisingly powerful manipulation of all around them and most particularly their mothers. In order for the babies to grow to psychological strength motherhood needs to be a delicate and ever-changing compromise between providing for them and responding to their attempts to control while at the same time containing and limiting their megalomania!

What seems to be an even more difficult compromise to achieve is that between the child growing to psychological health and the mother maintaining hers. There are two main difficulties with this negotiation. The first is to do with the inbuilt martyrdom which often receives external validation and encouragement. Many other people will respond positively to perfectly selfless mothering and so martyrdom, in the short term, can be very rewarding. It is, however, extremely depleting and therefore leaves the mother feeling empty, hollow and psychologically fragile before long. Anyone with a tendency to martyrdom needs to remember that in 'real' life martyrs often end up dead; psychological martyrs can feel like death too.

Our ability to give, psychologically, should be seen as a bank account. You can give that which you have already stored away, you can even give from an overdraft if you have enough security, but once the bank is empty you cannot give any more. Motherhood is distinctly less painful for the women who are able to keep their 'giving' account in credit and who can remember that love, caring and security need to be consistently given to them if they are going to be able to give it out to small children. It is also easy for mothers to give from extensive resources of caring early on in mothering only to find themselves left short when the second, third or fourth baby arrives, or when there is a family crisis, a death or another major upheaval. Life does not wait for your children to grow up before handing out other difficulties and depleting events with which tired and harassed mothers are meant to cope. And motherhood itself goes on for a very long time.

Mothers with small babies need to remember that in ten years' time they will still need some resources and not overspend too early. When my children were still small people kept telling me that 'it gets worse'. How could it get worse? I wondered. In retrospect I think it is a good idea to have a time-scale to parenting and to ration out available resources in a way that is kind to the mother as well as realistic to the child. It is so hard for martyrs to accept or seek kindness and yet mothers with young children need kindness and consideration more than any other group of adults in our community.

The second problem in the mother/baby compromise

comes from our ways of judging mothering. Society, having handed over the entire responsibility of mothering to women, can afford to have unreasonable expectations of what good mothering is. Hence messages that mothers should be constantly available, always put the baby's needs first, have no needs of their own and should aim towards a form of perfect relating with the baby abound. There is no mention of a failure and yet every mother recognises early in the process that, sometimes at least, she is failing. The baby will cry and she might not know why. Perhaps she cannot stop the baby crying. She may even be too tired to care if the baby continues to cry. Sometimes, because no one is meeting her own needs and, her resources are rapidly disappearing, she may be desperate, resentful, even raging. This can all be experienced as failure and as no one mentions the possibility of failing as a mother, individual women become wrapped up in a guilty certainty that they are the first and only mother to fail in this way. There has been psycho-analytic talk of 'good enough' mothering but quite what good enough consisted of has never been discussed. For many women anything short of perfection begins to feel like failure and they become caught in a spiral of trying ever harder to achieve the unachievable, and then becoming increasingly guilty with what they see as the worst failure of their lives.

'Good enough' mothering describes mothering that responds to enough of the baby's needs to allow that child a secure psychological base from which to develop its personality. It is not an absolute. Each child has different needs and responds to the care it receives in different ways. Some children are much more demanding than others, some appear almost insatiable in their demands, while others hardly ever cry and appear content with their lot in life even if that lot is relatively meagre. Some babies are angry at birth; perhaps the whole process of birth has already overwhelmed and outraged them. Others appeared interested or mildly surprised, but still more ready to face the world. To be a 'good enough' mother to a happy baby is a great deal more easy than to be 'good enough' to one of the crying, sick or never-satisfied variety. Most mothers fail to be 'good enough' some of the time, when they are tired, for instance, or when other events or relationships stress them beyond what is endurable. 'Good enough' should therefore be seen as a prolonged reflection over many years, an average of all the mothering that is offered. Women who reckon themselves not 'good enough' with babies are often inspired with adolescents. Most of all women should judge themselves against 'good enough' kindly if at all.

Paradoxically failing as a mother, overtly and without guilt, is a great success. It allows the fresh air of reality into the nursery previously stuffy with hallowed fantasies of perfect mothers. It allows both mother and baby space within the claustrophobia of those early days together. It is not the failure, but the guilt and ensuing depression that harms mother and baby.

Psychological failure is a normal part of all relationships because we can never be more than an approximate 'fit' to each other. Mothers cannot 'fit' each of their babies with anything more than imperfection. Mothers are not shapeless expendable blobs that can merge effortlessly with whatever genetic fate happens to throw at them, and we do neither mother nor baby any good by holding out unrealistic expectations that they would be if they were 'good' mothers. The compromise between mother and baby's needs is much more easily negotiated in the real world of commonplace and accepted failure than in the never-never land of perfectionist mothering. As one woman said to me, 'If I could just get rid of this guilt, I might feel like a normal person again!'

Many of our emotions are responses to what is happening in our life. It is more difficult to find happiness in circumstances of material or psychological deprivation. In many ways motherhood often does mean the presence of this double deprivation in women's lives and yet because it is meant to be a 'happy' event and one that most women feel they have 'chosen' they feel it is wrong to be depressed. Not only are women self-critical of their negative emotional response to motherhood, they also quickly discover that everyone else is highly critical of it too. This leads many women to cover up their feelings, to think of their feelings as bad or shameful and to deny them, to themselves as well as to others. Buried feelings do not go away, they lurk under the surface looking for some other way out. Some women are lucky enough to have friends, hobbies or work as 'vents' for the black side of mothering but those women who have no safety valves have an increasing build-up of pressure in their psyches. Many women have said to me, 'I just want to open my mouth and scream and scream to let all the bad feelings out.'

All mothers need time to acknowledge feelings, to have those feelings validated by others as reasonable and normal, and to see those feelings as directly connected to the lives they are leading. Changing styles of life in a way that is kinder to mothers eases a lot of the inner deprivation. It is, for instance, quite unrealistic to imagine that one adult can look after a baby (let alone several children) day in day out, twenty-four hours a day, without enormous self-deprivation. Some form of shared caring, be it within the circle of family or friends or paid help, can make an instant difference to feelings of exhaustion and emptiness in young mothers. A good night's sleep occasionally is essential for the mental health of each of us and yet most mothers with young children see this as an unobtainable luxury. What sort of society is this which allows young women to endure what is basically a form of torture, to see it as normal and even right that they should continue to endure without help? Realistic kindness to self is every bit as important a part of the new mother's life as caring for the baby.

Feelings of overwhelming sadness are a common reaction to loss of any sort, be it income or independence. For many the good side of mothering makes up for the losses, at least some of the time, and for mothers who have never had emotional or financial independence, nor gained any sort of self-knowledge prior to the birth, the losses may be insignificant when compared to the gains. However, an increasing number of women have begun to make adult lives for themselves, independent and enjoying it, prior to their first child and for this group motherhood represents a great loss, both of external parameters such as income and adult company, but also of inner space, time to do what you want, and ways of valuing self.

One woman described her experience to me: 'I felt as if I was falling into a hole much like Alice in Wonderland. Nothing made sense any more. I was not the boss, had no control, could make no decisions, and every second seemed full of something or somebody else apart from me. Within two weeks I had lost any sense of who or what I had ever been and I began to feel as if I had died. My tears were a form of grief at losing the me that I was familiar with.'

For women who have lost their mothers during childhood and adolescence this sense of loss and of being lost can be very intense. Even those daughters with heated and critical relationships with their mothers often find, to their surprise, that it is their mother they trust with their baby more than anyone else, including the father. In the early days, when it is hard to conquer anxieties long enough to let the baby go to a stranger for a few hours, most mothers find they are able to relinquish control, at least temporarily, to their mothers. One young mother said, 'I hated my mother; she had been violent and unpredictable with me and yet I found that I trust her completely with my daughter. I don't understand it, but it was as if there was still a strong bond . . . femaleness . . . that held us together and apart from everyone else.'

For the women who do not have this relationship to fall back on, or for those who have such distant or difficult relationships with their mothers that they cannot or will not ask for help, the sense of loss is accompanied by intense loneliness. They often experience a desperation for what they have lost in the past as well as an awareness of what is presently lacking in their lives. Substitute mums of any description, be they relatives or friends, can help to ease the intensity of the pain but many of these women need time away from the baby on a regular basis to explore their own wounds and heal.

Fiona's mother was killed in a car accident when she was 4. Three months after the birth of her daughter Fiona came to see me saying, 'I think that I have always had a badly healed wound resulting from my mother's death. Susie's birth has ripped that wound apart and I feel as if I might bleed to death.' She was giving a graphic description of her feeling that life was ebbing away from her and that without the person who had originally given her that life to protect her all was lost. Gradually she came to understand that her mother had given her much love during those first years and that it was a tragedy but not of her making that her mother had died. Realising that she had not 'killed' her mother with her normal aggressive feelings meant that she could begin to hope to survive motherhood herself.

Depression is also often the result of anger that becomes turned in against the self instead of being aimed at the person who has made us angry. Women still find it difficult to express anger and when they do express it in ways that society would consider appropriate for men, they are usually condemned as mad, bad or unwomanly. This is most particularly true of anger towards children, especially babies, and husbands.

It is considered wrong to be angry with babies because we all fear that hitting or killing them would be the inevitable result of admitting and then losing control of our anger. Babies are, however, very frustrating. They are also highly tuned to their mother's feelings and so when they sense that she is unwell, unhappy or distracted, they have an unfailing ability to find some way to re-engage her in order to reassure themselves. This means that babies are often most demanding when their mothers are least able to cope with those demands. When the baby's demands are combined with her own increasing fatigue, the mother may feel more angry than she can ever remember feeling before. We tend to hide these feelings from others because we know that they frighten us and assume, often correctly, that they will therefore frighten others too. The anger stays inside of mother; she then begins to criticise herself and feel a sense of guilt and failure.

Many depressed mothers will say that they are being very bad mothers when to the rest of the world they appear to be caring and responsible. The anger with the baby has been turned inside-out and is allowed to escape as anger with self. Shared care has the liberating opportunity for more than one adult to swap notes on the same baby and say, 'Isn't it annoying when . . . ?' In this way the tension and frustration can be shared and normalised, and become openly acceptable. Tension and frustration are understandable responses to a difficult baby. It is only when mothers are left alone, day after day, to cope without external support that these feelings seem insurmountable.

As well as feeling angry with their babies mothers also continue to experience the normal adult response of anger to other people who are damaging or frustrating to themselves as well as events and stresses that annoy us all. The baby is therefore not the sole focus of stress but an additional one, over and above all those experienced by all adults. Women with unhappy relationships, particularly with their partners or their own mothers, are most likely to become angry as the stresses of early parenthood overload the woman's coping strategies and the flaws in these relationships, upon which the woman might have hoped to rely, become more obvious. Many women feel abandoned in the experience of motherhood, alone in the early morning hours of feeding or soothing the baby, alone during the day, cut off from other adult stimulation, and alone at night because their partners are doing something 'more important', be that work, sport or a hobby, than be with them. Not surprisingly these women experience an intense anger at their perceived abandonment as well as feeling unable to rescue themselves from their painful situation.

When women express their distress to friends, relatives or caring agencies they are often told that it is not 'real' distress but merely their hormones 'acting up'. There are two flaws to such a diagnosis. Firstly pain is distressing whatever its cause and this sort of dismissive response often only serves to make the woman quieter about her feelings in future. Secondly there is increasing evidence that we should be more circumspect about believing hormonal explanations for women's feelings. A small number of women probably do experience a variety of emotional problems connected to hormonal changes in their bodies. However, they are in a minority and all trials and research to date suggests that there is no definite link between a particular hormone and a particular feeling. Hence women interpret what is happening inside their bodies with the same distinctive personal bias with which they interpret external events.

The only exception to this is five-day 'blues' after the birth of the baby. It does seem as if this experience has some connection with rapidly falling levels of progesterone. But depression is a common phenomena after any major physical trauma and 'baby blues' is therefore probably only partially hormonally determined. More importantly there is no evidence for arguing a hormonal theory for the wide variety of mental suffering after childbirth nor for the fact that that suffering often continues for a lengthy period of time.

The results of all these psychological experiences are revealed in statistics on illness in mothers of young children. (These figures should not be read as what is normal for women having children, but rather as what is the emotional reality for women in this culture at this time attempting to be 'good' mothers. In many ways they suggest that we are being extraordinarily careless with the feelings of these women.) Using strict psychiatric criteria, 15–20 per cent of mothers are affected by new episodes of mental illness within a year of childbirth. If those criteria are relaxed a little to include more transient disturbances the rate rises to between 30–40 per cent. This means that women run five times the risk of mental illness in the first year of their baby's life and an astounding sixteen times the risk of serious (psychotic) illness within the first three months compared to at any other time in their lives. Out of 1,000 live births, in a study in Nottingham, two mothers were admitted to hospital with a psychotic illness while another five were diagnosed as psychotic but treated in the community; forty mothers had other major psychiatric diagnoses, for instance mania or psychotic depression, and a further 100 had 'minor' psychiatric disorder, a form of intense and severe distress.

For 85 per cent of the mothers diagnosed as having psychotic or severe disorders it is the first episode of such an experience and often comes completely unexpectedly and very suddenly. In this way it is more like post-operative psychosis, that is, a reaction to a major life event.

There is some indication that this kind of presentation of the mother's inner distress is related to family history. This can make the situation difficult for the whole family to deal with, awakening memories in the woman's mother of her own frightening experiences. Sometimes this enables her to be supportive to her daughter but tragically it often seems to have an adverse effect on their relationship, as if the reappearance of psychotic illness is perceived by the family as a failure or a weakness of which both mother and daughter should be ashamed. As a society we tend to reflect that fear and condemnation of mental illness, and yet in my experience the people who do react to stress in this way are often amongst the more gentle, caring and sensitive people in our community. Interestingly doctors' wives have a high rate of psychotic illness.

When psychotic, women experience a sense of confusion and disorientation. They may become disinhibited and make little sense when they talk. Often forgetful of their own needs they become rapidly dehydrated. A psychotic woman will often have moments, even hours, of feeling back to normal before the frightening experience overwhelms her again. She may have hallucinations when she hears people condemning her and she may fear plots against herself and the baby. Such mothers often continue to show interest in and caring towards their children even when acutely distressed and confused themselves. Good immediate care, with high intensity nursing, can rectify the crisis quickly. Even with medication the flow of breast milk can be maintained so that as soon as medication ceases the mother can return to breast-feeding. The presence of drugs excreted via breast milk means that mothers cannot breast-feed their babies in the short term. They may also feel too restless and agitated and staff may experience high levels of anxiety in allowing these mothers to feed their infants. Specially trained staff are needed who can cope with their own anxieties and continue to maximise the closeness of mother and baby in a way that is sensitive to the needs of both. Allowing mothers to bring their babies with them into hospital means that most mothers will consent to admission. As long as reasonable facilities exist and kindness is used in helping them with their crisis, only a small minority are admitted to hospital under an order of the Mental Health Act.

Eighty per cent of women who have this experience do so within two weeks of delivery, i.e. it is an acute reaction to overwhelming stress in susceptible women. Having a Caesarean section seems to increase the likelihood of such a reaction, presumably because it increases the enormity of the life event. Only one in five of those women who experience this distress with their first baby will experience it with subsequent babies, although one in two are at risk of becoming ill at some point in their future lives if over-stressed. This underlines the importance of discussing the future with each woman and her family to ensure that she receives adequate support and emotional help to avoid further difficulties. It also shows how important it is to develop 'user-friendly' psychiatric facilities that encourage families to seek help as early as is needed without any stigma.

Women who become depressed are by everyone's descriptions 'very ordinary women'. Those who become depressed within a month of the birth tend to be the most seriously disturbed, while those for whom depression creeps in slowly tend to get missed by health visitors and GPs because they describe their experiences in ways that are different to descriptions of 'normal' depression in adults. There is also a tendency to downgrade the severity of any diagnosis of mental distress in women as if we have stereotypal images of what level of distress is acceptable. This downgrading is particularly apparent in young women and in women from minority cultures. Suffering experienced by those who are different to ourselves usually appears less extreme or important in some way. Hence men tend to downgrade suffering in women and there is less sympathy between different cultures for the others' suffering, combined with difficulties in communicating that suffering in the first place. This tendency is important for women, especially women from ethnic minorities, when they try to attract the attention of the helping agencies to their distress, as the majority of those agencies are white and male dominated in how they diagnose and react to that distress. However, the severity of distress often experienced by mothers of young babies seems to be more intense than other forms of depression in young adults, when recognised and explored.

The most common sign of their depression is complaining of their worthlessness as mothers. These complaints tend to be accepted at face value rather than compared with reality and questioned, hence the mother's sadness escapes without comment. Many women report a state of 'feeling nothing' for themselves, their babies or for anyone or anything. They may worry about the baby, going over and over safety precautions such as washing out feeding bottles many times more than necessary. A classical sign of all depression is waking early in the morning. As all mothers, whether depressed or not, tend to be woken early anyway this sign can easily get overlooked and yet often demonstrates the severity of the mother's distress. Also typical is a fluctuation of mood during the day, feeling worse in the mornings and then gradually lifting as the day goes on. As men tend to spend time with their families only in the evening they can be completely unaware of just how seriously depressed the woman has become. Many also turn a blind eye to the level of distress, being frightened by what they see and not having any idea what they can do about it. Women are especially at risk of becoming severely depressed if they have had a Caesarean section and an earlier major loss (particularly of a previous child or of their mother). Again medication may become necessary but self-help groups, non-directive counselling, psychotherapy and instruction in a realistic style of mothering are probably all more important for the future happiness of the woman concerned.

A large number of women, up to almost half of new mothers, experience a mild to moderate form of depression during the first year of their baby's life. There are many risk factors involved in making women vulnerable at this time and such risks tend to become cumulative, so that most women can manage to cope with some but not a lot of problems, pre-delivery, during delivery and afterwards. These risk factors are no respecters of social class and many of them can be reduced by planning and improving care and support.

Risk factors before birth include early deprivation of the mother in her own childhood, being single, being a very young or older mother, having a history of mental illness in the mother's past or in her family, marital and family discord (relationships with other women seem to have a strongly protective function against the adverse effects of marital discord), loss of the last baby or prolonged infertility investigations prior to conception. Uncertainty about continuing the pregnancy and exploration of the possibility of an abortion which is later rejected also increase the woman's vulnerability once the baby is delivered.

During the later days of pregnancy and birth over-anxiety about the welfare of the baby by medical or nursing staff, anxiety or depression in the mother immediately prior to birth, prolonged admissions to hospital during the pregnancy, Caesarean section, and any major life event, like moving house, in the late days of pregnancy or early days post-birth, all place the mother under more extreme stress.

In the early days of motherhood illness in either the mother or baby or both and major life events such as death, unemployment or marital breakdown often overwhelm women when they are at their most vulnerable. For this group of women self-help groups to increase self-esteem and protect against social isolation, counselling to ease unrealistic expectations and psychotherapy to help explore longer-standing problems are all much more useful than anything conventional psychiatry has to offer.

One form of distress that often misses description simply because it is so commonplace is the extent of feelings of anxiety that new mothers experience for their babies, themselves and their relationships. One mother told me, 'I was afraid to push the pram down our road because I felt as if an articulated lorry was going to come pounding down on us both.' Considering that she lived in a quiet village far from main roads this was clearly not a likely possibility and yet the anxiety surrounding her fears was very real indeed. The world had suddenly become a threatening place where neither she nor the child could feel safe. This sort of experience is very common and reflects a complex mixture of a heightened awareness of the real dangers of the external world, which suddenly seem to be all around, and also of the dangers internally. New motherhood reveals the depths of her unconscious mind to the woman, in her emotions, reactions and dreams. Much of this material is frightening and even horrific. For those women who cannot believe that they harbour such thoughts or feelings there is a need to project them into the outside world. However, if you project all the 'inner devils' into the world around you it does, indeed, become a frightening place.

Presumably there was a time in the evolution of our species when high levels of anxiety in mothers was very protective for both mother and baby in their truly hostile world. Despite the news constantly telling us how dangerous our present world is, it can hardly compare with the dangers of several thousands of years ago or even five hundred years back. Motherhood, being a primitive experience that connects us directly to those distant generations, probably reawakens that primitive anxiety which may well seem entirely out of proportion with the real dangers faced by new mothers and their children in this day and age. There is little point in trying to reason with the early sensations of maternal anxiety. Many women experience it as an emotion far beyond the rational. Sometimes it is so extreme that mothers cannot bear to leave their babies for a moment and sometimes it is prolonged beyond the early days of the child's life, as if the mother cannot be soothed by the real safety around her into dropping some of her fears. Sometimes, sadly, the woman's environment is, in reality, not safe but she finds it difficult or impossible to explain the reality of the circumstances and so presents her anxiety only as a plea for help.

Anxiety is often described as the most painful and wearing of all our emotions. Because it is such an unbearable experience people will do all they can to avoid feeling it and soon discover ways of distancing the feeling or avoiding it. By placing all the fears into some part of the outside world and then avoiding that part the anxiety can be controlled. It remains as 'the black dog that is following me, behind, out of sight, but always there', as one woman described her feelings. 'I cannot go into town because then it would catch me.' The 'black dog' of her terrors was that anxious part of herself which caused her so much anguish. A life can soon become narrowed within 'safe' confines in order to avoid the dreaded anxiety but then the woman risks becoming increasingly cut off and isolated, leading to increasing pressures from within herself and further breakthoughs of the anxiety. The woman with the 'black dog' said, 'One day I had to turn round and face what it was that was so frightening. When I did I discovered that it only existed inside of me . . . in fact it really did not exist at all.'

It is important for all women who experience these problems in their early days of mothering to remember that they are not alone. Far from it! They are probably in the majority. In order to look at ways of 'curing' this distress we presently place much emphasis on 'curing' the individual woman. This ignores the enormity of the problem in the whole of society, across all social and economic barriers. For a society to make mothering such a demoralising business for its young women seems extraordinarily self-defeating. We would need a major reassessment about the value of mothers and children before any change in the important external factors is likely to be achieved. I recently heard a group of young mothers joking and one said, 'When the boat sinks, and they say women and children first into the lifeboats, it is just because the men want to see if the lifeboats sink before taking them over for their own use!' This hollow joke caused laughter with a sharp edge in the group and there were many knowing nods of 'Yes, that's just what it feels like'. The sense of being left to drown is strong in young mothers today. It is not their fantasy, nor is it due to any inherent weakness in themselves as women and as people. Indeed, at almost any gathering of young mothers I often feel humbled by the extraordinary strength, courage and generosity of spirit that each woman demonstrates at the same time as belittling herself and her role in society. Too often, the women themselves lose sight of their great value as they are swamped by the much more jaded values of a competitive society strongly motivated by power and money. New mothers are made miserable by this external false value-system which is demonstrated to them in the politics, the social fabric, the advertising, and the economic structure which pervades their everyday life. The mothers who can remain happiest are those who can stretch their understandings and inner certainties down into their female roots, own and appreciate themselves as women and appreciate other women too. Women who see the external values as entirely secondary, mostly male and presently wrong, often feel strengthened by the experiences of motherhood as if it underlines their inner certainties of something more important than those external values. Hence women with a good group of women friends who share their lives with honesty and humour, in a warm appreciation both of strengths and foibles, tend to survive the experience of motherhood a great deal more easily than those women who give over-valuation to men and male external values, and alongside that denigrate other women and the most preciously female parts of themselves.

The problem is that such an attitude takes inner certainty, strength and energy. It involves a constant external fight against all that is spoken in the outside world as well as an internal fight with many of the values fed to us by a society which determines that we will abide by those external values or else. Motherhood, particularly late pregnancy, birth and the first year of a child's life, leave a woman psychologically vulnerable. Her physical resources are continuously drained with little time for respite and her psychological boundaries are breeched in a way that makes her vulnerable to any hint of criticism and rejected and also susceptible to anyone who wishes to 'brainwash' her about how she should behave or what she should be. Having two or more children leaves women in this 'open' state for a number of years and, at the time, it feels like a permanent state. Women with two or three small children often say, 'I have always felt like this and I am always going to feel like this', demonstrating just how lost in the experience they are. In this state it is too easy for the mother's values to be overwhelmed by the values of her husband, her family, her community or society as a whole. In losing the sense of value of self and adopting the values of others we lose our tether in life, our sense of rightness, direction, structure and wholeness. We lose ourselves and often, as part of that process, women lose each other.

Hence in a situation where the company of other women of all ages is demonstrated to be the single most healthy resource for young mothers we find ourselves in a culture which limits and even prevents this contact. Houses are built to separate, life styles with enforced 'career' movement divide, husbands wanting their dinners on the table or the house empty of anyone except their wife and children when they get home dictate estrangement. This all adds to the fact that making contact with other adults while a small child is awake and in the near vicinity is extremely difficult and always likely to be fragmented and unsatisfying from the adults' point of view. Babies and small children see their mother's friends as rivals for her time and energy. Thus the response often heard of 'but women spend all day together' misses the point. The need is for real adult-to-adult psychological communication, a sense of being heard and understood, to validate our own experience. Just spending time together, surrounded by children making unpredictable demands, having emergencies of great variety and needing for their own psychological satisfaction to prevent the adults communicating is not the same as making adult-to-adult connection.

Many women seek this in the evening from their partners only to find that such engagement disappoints both adults. His life is very different to hers. Both will feel that their way is harder and will listen with a slightly critical and hostile ear to the other's day . . . 'Well, if you think that's hard, you should hear what I've had to do.' For both adults involved such sharing often becomes a battlefield rather than a time of mutual rewarding and caring. Only couples who really share much of both the caring of children and the external battle for survival can hope to satisfy each other's need for adult-to-adult communication at this time. It is asking the unreasonable from any other form of relationship. Despite this countless couples sit alone and locked into their own painful enmity, unaware of the fact that their battle is not an individual one based on their own frailties so much as a universal difficulty in understanding the pleasures and pitfalls of lives very different from our own. At times of stress we need to share like with like. The excitement of sharing differences occurs when we are relaxed and unstressed by other factors.

In summary, then, pregnancy, childbirth and child-rearing cause a complex reaction in the mother's psyche which is connected to the physical trauma and exhaustion and to the fact that her inner boundaries are breeched in a way that makes her less able to defend herself from both the external world and also from whatever lurks in her internal world of memories, dreams and fears. In this vulnerable psychological state she is not only still exposed to all that the world throws at adults day by day but also the enormous extra stress of a new and demanding small person in her life who is profoundly narcissistic. All this happens in the context of a society with entirely unreasonable ideas on how good mothers should be and which does nothing to reward mothers however good they are. Small wonder that many women find this an intolerable mixture. Much greater miracle that most women survive, grow and learn, become humorous about the experience and look back and say 'I am glad to have done it'. Our society should be grateful indeed for the extent of all that pain . . . Mothers' Day should probably rate alongside Remembrance Day as times when we remember those who give part or all of themselves for others and for the good of society generally.

10

DREAMS AND REALITIES

We each have a need to idealise relationships and the roles we and important others play in those relationships. This need represents an early part of our development when it was too threatening and complex to understand the ambivalent . . . good and bad . . . nature of all relationships. That earliest and most idealised of all relationships is therefore with our mothers. Idealisation can come in may forms. The most straightforward is simply to say that both your mother and the mothering you receive were perfect and that all mothering needs to be carried out in exactly the same way as that you received in order to be similarly perfect. More complex is to feel that everything that happened to you was wrong and that the ideal is therefore the complete reverse of what you experienced. Most of us sway between these two extremes, believing both to be true to some extent.

What we say, consciously, about our mother and the mothering we received may be quite different to either what we feel unconsciously or to what any external valuation of that experience might decide. It is possible for individuals to 'whitewash' their early life experience so as to preserve the good image of their mother or to see everything in the blackest of terms when in reality their experience was quite normal. We may be only half aware of these discrepancies in what we say and what we feel and sometimes we have no idea at all as to the extent of the discrepancy.

Parenthood throws new light, psychologically, on that earlier experience and often allows mothers a chance to re-live much of what previously transpired emotionally. In this way their mothers' feelings and behaviour become more real and understandable and these women are then able to make adult and appropriate judgments on that experience of being mothered. Men have less chance to make this fundamental readjustment because they tend to be protected from the real experiences of raising children to a considerable degree. Hence the majority of men pursue adult life with their child's view of mothering relatively untouched by adult experience. It is this view which is most reflected in our society and accounts for why much of what is expected of mothers is impossible for a single adult to achieve with consistency. As women tend to be separated from each other during the early years of this experience, and tend not to be honest about the extent of their perceived failures to meet expectations even if they do talk with other women during this phase, there is a failure to describe the experience of mothering accurately as an adult experience with appropriate and realistic expectations. Each mother knows individually what the experience is like but is uncertain as to whether she is abnormal or not. As the supposed normality is perfection and as all mothers fail to meet that expectation they are likely to feel abnormally bad as mothers and therefore particularly unwilling to share honestly what the experience has been like for themselves.

The notion of ideals extends beyond our feelings of proper mothering into areas such as relationships, particularly marriage, and the development and innate qualities of each baby. Women are held to be as responsible for these as they are for achieving perfect mothering. Hence not only is mothering judged against an ideal (and it is a different ideal for each individual) but also bound up in that ideal are the attainments of the baby and the quality of her relationship with the child's father. Hence 'good mothering leads to happy and accomplished baby' is a commonly held belief and conversely an unhappy baby who is late reaching the milestones of walking and potty training, and later reading and polite manners, is believed to have been subjected to bad mothering. Similarly there is an equation between 'good mothering' of the baby and 'good mothering' of the father. The implication is that these two are directly related and that women who make good mothers will, of course, also satisfy their partners' needs. These equations tend to ignore the individual characteristics of both the baby and the man.

Babies are not blank sheets on which the mother can write her own script from birth, and men are certainly not without their own foibles and difficulties, many of which suddenly become apparent with the birth of the first child.

There is a tendency to believe that the goals society sets for its members today are in some way concrete and correct. This leaves little space for individuals to be different and yet still regarded as valid. In order to be recognised as a 'good' mother one of the functions society requires is that mothers mould their children to as close a match to society's ideals as possible. Even in a peaceful society with democratic ideals this is often difficult. Children may not be clever, physically co-ordinated, attractive, creative or even very nice. Some of this can be rectified with love, example and consistency, to the child's advantage as well as society's. But what of the behaviour which society wants from its citizens but a mother might not want from her child, such as, stereotypically, aggression in boys and passivity in girls? What of the behaviour the child is incapable of producing because of its innate restrictions? And what of behaviour that society and father condone and which is an obscenity to the mother? Ideals seem superficially to provide an answer to the troubling problems of living with much that is contradictory and paradoxical and yet living towards these ideals, cultural and within a lifetime changeable as they are, adds much chaos and conflict to family life.

Given the strong psychological pull of the hopes for an ideal relationship, ideal mothering, ideal baby, ideal marriage and happy-ever-after endings how can we hope to write a more realistic story about ourselves? It is surprising to each generation in its turn that it cannot tell or warn today's teenagers of the problems they will meet in marriage and parenthood. It seems as if the the only hope we have of learning is to do it ourselves. Even then it is only if we take responsibility for the experience and the outcome of such adventures that we may hope to learn from them. Many adults survive years of multiple marriages and many young children, and yet fail to learn about themselves from the experience because they always attach the blame and responsibility for each mistake and failure to someone or something else.

Recently there have been discussions about whether some form of social education should be included in all basic curriculum. This has begun to ease its way into the classroom in the face of opposition from many adults who see it as a way of brainwashing children and pulling them away from the 'ideals' of family life. It is precisely that family life as non-ideal but real to which the teaching should be addressed. Instead the ignorance continues, and today, as thirty years ago, intelligent girls in their last year of school look to marriage and maternity to provide their fulfilment and security while boys look to careers, money and status as a means of personal fulfilment. For as long as the split exists so will the disappointment and disillusionment of young new mothers overwhelmed by the rude reality and the sad breakdowns of men in their late thirties and forties who awake from their external successes to find that personal fulfilment has escaped them. Strange we should argue in Parliament to preserve Latin in our schools and yet have such ambivalent thoughts on preparing children for much that is central in adult life.

Some would say that parenthood is necessarily disillusioning. Without such an experience an individual cannot take the next step on the slow path towards personal maturity. The process by which our hopes and expectations disintegrate, and through which we then reconstruct them differently to allow for what we have just learnt, is an important feature in the development of our personalities from the day we are born. Certainly the experience of having to put someone else first is an important one for all human beings and it is a sad person who goes through life only putting themselves first. Such selflessness has to be coupled with realism and with self-survival, however, or it can become as pathological as the other extreme. The mother's prime task is to survive as best she can within the need to be relatively selfless for a long time. Human babies take many years to become anything like mature and the giving from mother to child continues in different forms throughout that time. Mothers need to maintain flexible resources for themselves and their families. To maintain self is an important part of the adult planning needed to maintain some degree of selflessness.

Finally, parenthood is a unique journey for each person who undertakes it. The journeys have much in common and the travellers have much to gain from honest sharing and mutual support, but each psychological journey is a new relationship with a new and unique individual and as such is unknowable until it has happened. Much that happens in life is only understood in retrospect and never is this more true than with parenting. Hence each traveller embarks with hopes, dreams, expectations, hazy knowledge from the odd guide book or two, and in the complex confusion of relationships and a society which have yet to 'come clean' about anything approaching reality as most find it.

If there is a true message about parenting it is that it lasts for ever. I have met women, in their eighties, who told me of miscarriages or illegal abortions of tiny foetuses sixty years ago or more. Each of those events started a clock ticking within the woman's life. Although the child had never lived for society it had never died for its mother. At the other extreme mothering and a sense of motherhood extends far beyond the infant's childhood. Hence conception is one of the very few events that changes the course of an individual's life for ever. That course can be modified after the event but it cannot be undone.

The new course can be good, bad or indifferent. For most it is a complex mixture of all three. Motherhood is basically a relationship and not a career. It cannot be researched or studied for, there are no exams, no accolades, no financial rewards and no promotion. However, for a majority of women it is with their children that they have the crucial relationships in their lives, closely followed in intensity and importance by their relationships with their own mothers. Hence the good is more wonderful and ecstatic, the bad more terrible and terrifying and the indifferent worrying and full of guilt. One mother summed up motherhood to me as '10 per cent wonder, 30 per cent guilt, 50 per cent exhaustion, 5 per cent satisfaction and 5 per cent "Thank goodness I embarked on this. I would have been a lesser person without my children."'

As with all accounts of experience and theory, this as much as any other is a personal contribution. It is about myself and the women with whom I have had the privilege of sharing experiences over many years. It may be that you recognise yourself in some of the contents and even find some of the conclusions helpful in making sense of your own experience. Equally you may find that it does not reflect your experience at all and that you even feel 'at odds' with what I have said. If I have a surviving dream about motherhood, it is that women will come to be able to express themselves about the experience honestly and without guilt or embarrassment. That we may disagree about the nature of the experience is healthy. Neither should any woman feel that all the blame for confusion and conflict lies with society or with her partner, who is often the representative of that society within the home. In the end changes in the external world only have meaning to those individuals who struggle with their internal pro- gramming, looking for the 'bugs' and seeking new knowledge, strength and experience to overcome them. Until we are brave enough to speak clearly about the realities of mothering across the wide spectrum of experienced opinion we cannot blame society for having crazy mixed-up notions and fantasies.

I will never forget my surprise at just how endless my first baby's demands were, nor will I ever forget just how ill-prepared I was to meet those demands. Sometimes when he was lying in his cot resembling a young Gandhi (because it took me months to perfect nappy-folding!) I would look at this fragile wonder I had created with disbelief. The burden of responsibility often felt like a physical load on my back. At times I was sure that I was the worst mother in recorded history. I felt torn by raging emotions over his safety, un- willing to leave him alone, listening to his breathing through the night and yet equally longing to be free again from the suffocating burden of motherhood. At a workshop recently women were asked to put a single word to their experiences as new mothers and the words chosen were 'devastation, interruption, crisis, turmoil, rage, no privacy and deprivation'. Despite these words each woman agreed that the experience had an almost mystical quality which they would not have missed. I would agree with all of that.

I can remember the night when the magic struck me most forcibly. It was 4.00 a.m., the baby was awake, feeding; I was awake, revising from a textbook for my Final exams, just a few weeks away; my husband was asleep in the far corner of the room. I felt adrift from all that I had previously known and angry with the rest of the world for being asleep when I was awake. I suddenly realised that Ben had stopped sucking and was looking at me as if to try and work out what kind of mother he had landed himself with. I saw that his eyes were now focused and remarkably shrewd. And I felt his uncertainty with as much force as my own. We eyed each other with suspicion, with adoration and with amusement. His younger brother years later wrote as the answer to a school essay entitled 'What is a mother', 'Mothers are people who are reasonable for half of the time.' Of course they must have wished, and probably still do, that I was a little more perfect. There have been times when I have certainly wished that they were a little more perfect! But we are landed with each other; that is the reality we work with and for the most part that reality is surprisingly easier than any ideal fantasy.

My two children have instructed me in the arts of motherhood. They have taught me more than a million textbooks could. When I felt they were leading me adrift I fell back on my intuitive roots. Nothing can be taken for granted in parenthood. But I know that under their 'tutorage' I have become more self-critical and more honest about my limitations; they have taught me to relax and be more open about my feelings – a necessity rather than a virtue. In the end their very presence, questioning and demanding as it is, has made me more confident about myself. They continually take me on a guided tour of my limits, physical, emotional, and intellectual, and having demonstrated these, revealing my inadequacy, they then proceed to love me despite everything. Hopefully such love will always be tempered with the knowledge that I am only 50 per cent reasonable! Without them and the many like them this book would have been neither necessary nor possible. Ben, Sam, and children everywhere, thank you for teaching the adults who give up a great deal to teach you.

FURTHER READING

Adams, C. T. and Winston, K. T., *Mothers at Work*, New York, Longman, 1980.

Arms, S., *Immaculate Deception: A New Look at Women and Childbirth in America*, Boston, Houghton Mifflin Company, 1975.

Baruch, G. K. and Barnett, R. C. 'Adult Daughters' Relationships with Their Mothers', *Journal of Marriage and the Family*, 45, pp. 601–6, 1983.

Barnett, R. C. and Baruch, G. K., 'Women's Involvement in Multiple Roles and Psychological Distress', *Journal of Personality and Social Psychology*, 49, pp. 135–45, 1985.

Beard, Mary Ritter, *On Understanding Women*, New York, Grosset & Dunlap, 1931.

de Beauvoir, Simone, *The Second Sex*, Harmondsworth, Penguin, 1972.

Bennetts, A. B. and Lubric, R. W., 'The Free-Standing Birth Centre', *The Lancet*, 1, 378–80, 1982.

Bernard, Jessie, *The Future of Marriage*, New York, World Publishing, 1972.

Bernard, Jesse, *Women, Wives, Mothers*, Chicago, Aldine, 1975.

Broverman, I., Broverman, D., Clarkson, F., Rosenkrantz, P. and Vogal, S., 'Sex-Role Stereotypes and Clinical Judgements of Mental Health', *Journal of Consulting and Clinical Psychology*, 34, pp. 1–7, 1970.

Chesler, Phyllis, *Women and Madness*, London, Allen Lane, 1972.

Chodorow, Nancy, *The Reproduction of Mothering: Psychoanalysis and the Sociology of Gender*, Berkeley, University of California Press, 1978.

Cohen, R., 'A Comparative Study of Women Choosing Two Different Childbirth Alternatives', *Birth*, 9, pp. 13–20, 1982.

Daly, Mary, *Beyond God the Father: Toward a Philosophy of Women's Liberation*, Boston, Beacon Press, 1973.

Daly, Mary, *Gyn/Ecology: The Metaethics of Radical Feminism*, London, Women's Press, 1979.

Dworkin, Andrea, *Women Hating*, New York, E. P. Dutton, 1974.

Eakins, Pamela, 'The Rise of the Free-Standing Birth Center: Principles and Practice', *Women and Health*, 9, 4, pp. 49–64, Winter 1984.

Eichenbaum, Luise and Orbach, Susie, *Outside In . . . Inside Out*, Harmondsworth, Penguin, 1982.

Eichenbaum, Luise and Orbach, Susie, *What Do Women Want?* London, Fontana, 1984.

Eichenbaum, Luise and Orbach, Susie, *Understanding Women*, Harmondsworth, Penguin, 1985.

Ellman, Mary, *Thinking about Women*, New York, Harcourt Brace Jovanovich, 1968, London, Virago, 1979.

Engels, Frederick, *The Origins of the Family*, New York, Pathfinder Press, 1972.

Fischer, L. R. 'Transitions in the Mother-Daughter Relationship', *Journal of Marriage and the Family*, 43, pp. 613–22, 1981.

Friday, Nancy, *My Mother, My Self*, London, Fontana, 1979.

Friedan, Betty, *The Feminine Mystique*, New York, Norton, 1963.

Gerson, Mary-Joan, 'The Prospect of Parenthood for Women and Men', *Psychology of Women Quarterly*, 10.1, pp. 49–62, 1986.

Gove, W. and Tudor, J., 'Adult Sex Roles and Mental Illness', *American Journal of Sociology*, 78, 812–35, 1973.

Greer, Germaine, *The Female Eunuch*, London, McGibbon & Kee, 1970.

Greer, Germaine, *Sex and Destiny: The Politics of Human Fertility*, London, Secker & Warburg, 1984.

Hamill, L., 'Wives as Sole and Joint Breadwinners', *Government Economic Service Working Papers*, No. 13, London, HMSO.

Hamilton Cicely, *Marriage as a Trade*, London, Women's Press, 1981.

Hammer, S., *Daughters and Mothers: Mothers and Daughters*, London, Hutchinson, 1976.

Howell, Edith and Bayes, Margaret (eds), *Women and Mental Heath*, New York, Basic Books, 1981.

Kaplan, Barbara, 'A Psychobiological Review of Depression During Pregnancy', *Psychology of Women Quarterly*, 10.1, pp. 35–48, 1986.

Kitzinger, Sheila, *The Experience of Childbirth*, London, Gollancz, 1962.

Kitzinger, Sheila and Davis, J. A. (eds), *The Place of Birth*, Oxford University Press, 1978.

Knox, Kay, 'Women's Identity: Self-Psychology's New Promise', *Women and Therapy*, 4.3, pp. 57–69, Fall 1985.

Lemkan, Jeanne, 'Reflections on Selflessness in the Lives of

Women', *Women and Therapy*, 3.1, pp. 31–6, Spring 1984.

Leppert, Phyllis, 'The Effect of Pregnancy on Adolescent Growth and Development', *Women and Health*, 9, 2/3, pp. 65–79, 1985.

Letts, P., *Double Struggle: Sex Discrimination and One-Parent Families*, London, National Council for One Parent Families, 1983.

Macfarlane, A., *The Psychology of Childbirth*, London, Fontana, 1977.

Macintyre, S., 'Who Wants Babies? The Social Construction of "Instincts" ', in Barker, D. L. and Allen, S., *Sexual Divisions and Society*, London, Tavistock, 1976.

Miller, Jean Baker, *Toward a New Psychology of Women*, Harmondsworth, Penguin, 1978.

Mitchell, J. and Oakley, A. (eds), *The Rights and Wrongs of Women*, Harmondsworth, Penguin, 1976.

Moss, P. and Plewis, I., 'Mental Distress in Mothers of Pre-School Children in Inner London', *Psychological Medicine*, 7, pp. 641–52, 1977.

Myrdal, A. and Klein, V., *Women's Two Roles: Home and Work*, London, Routledge and Kegan Paul, 1956.

Oakley, Ann, *Women Confined: Towards a Sociology of Childbirth*, Oxford, Martin Robertson, 1980.

Oakley, Ann, *Subject Women*, London, Fontana, 1982.

Oakley, Ann, *From Here to Maternity*, London, Pelican, 1986.

O'Brien, Mary, *The Politics of Reproduction*, Boston, Routledge and Kegan Paul, 1981.

Phillips, Angela and Rakusen, Jill, *Our Bodies Ourselves*, Harmondsworth, Penguin, 1978.

Ravetz J., 'When Mother Breaks Down', *Social Work Today*, 13.21.14, 1982.

Rich, Adrienne, *Of Woman Born: Motherhood as Experience and Institution*, New York, Norton, 1977.

Rudd, Nancy and McKenry, Patrick, 'Family Influences on the Job Satisfaction of Employed Mothers', *Psychology of Women Quarterly*, 10.4, pp. 363–71, 1986.

Rutter, M., *Maternal Deprivation Reassessed*, Harmondsworth, Penguin, 1972.

Sears, R. R. Rau, L. and Alpert, R., *Identification and Childrearing*, California, Stanford University Press, 1965.

Sholomskas, Diane and Richey, Cheryl, 'The Influence of Mother–Daughter Relationships on Women's Sense of Self and Current Role Choices', *Psychology of Women Quarterly*, 10.2, pp. 171–82, 1986.

Smith, Dorothy and David, Sara, *Women Look at Psychiatry*, Vancouver, Vancouver University Press, 1975.

Stewart, F. H. *et al.*, *My Body, My Health: The Concerned Woman's Guide to Gynaecology*, New York, John Wiley, 1979.

Thompson, L. and Walker, A., 'Mothers and Daughters: Aid Patterns and Attachment', *Journal of Marriage and the Family*, 46, pp. 313–22, 1984.

Tilley, L. A. and Scott, J. W., *Women, Work and the Family*, New York, Holt, Rinehart and Winston, 1978.

Walker, Alexis; Thompson, Linda and Morgan, Carolyn, 'Two Generations of Mothers and Daughters: Role Position and Interdependence', *Psychology of Women Quarterly*, 11.2, pp. 195–208, 1987.

Warner, M., *Alone of All Her Sex: The Myth and Cult of the Virgin Mary*, London, Weidenfeld and Nicolson, 1976.

Weissman, M. M. and Kleram, G. L., 'Sex Differences and the Epidemiology of Depression', *Archives of General Psychiatry*, 34, pp. 98–111, 1977.

Welburn, V., *Postnatal Depression*, London, Fontana, 1980.

Winnicott, D., *The Child, the Family and the Outside World*, Harmondsworth, Penguin, 1964.

Zaretsky, E., *Capitalism, the Family and Personal Life*, New York, Harper and Row, 1976.

INDEX

Some other Pandora books you might enjoy:

THE MIDWIFE CHALLENGE

Edited by Sheila Kitzinger

Sheila Kitzinger has asked midwives from around the world to explore the current upheavals taking place internationally in maternity care.

Midwives are pioneering a new approach to childbirth. Traditionally seen as incompetent, ignorant, meddlesome and superstitious 'grannies', midwives now pose the greatest ever challenge to today's high-tech and conveyer-belt obstetrics.

Midwives are concerned about the quality of emotional care given to pregnant women. They are demanding that all women have the right to a one-to-one relationship with a midwife who can give her continuous care – through pregnancy, birth and after her baby is born. Internationally they face stiff opposition from the medical profession and doctors who will fight tooth and nail to retain complete control of childbirth. In many countries, midwives have been relegated to the status of obstetric nurses; only in a few places are they recognised as professionals in their own right.

With contributions from midwives in Australia, Bangladesh, Britain, Canada, Denmark, Finland, France, Guatemala, the Netherlands and the USA, *The Midwife Challenge* compares the position of midwives in different medical systems, in industrialised and developing countries, the problems they face and their hopes for the future. This is a book not only for midwives themselves and health workers, but for any woman who has ever had a baby or intends to have one.

Sheila Kitzinger, MBE, is a social anthropologist and author of best-selling books on childbirth and female sexuality.

0 86358 235 4

£5.95 pbk

YOUR LIFE AFTER BIRTH

Exercises and Meditations for the First Year of Motherhood

Paddy O'Brien

This positive and practical handbook draws on women's own accounts of their post-natal feelings and experiences, and provides a comprehensive programme of relaxation, guided fantasy, assertiveness and self-defence to help you grow stronger emotionally as well as physically.

It provides practical, mental and physical exercises to help you cope with tiredness and the new demands on your time and emotions, and to make positive plans for *yourself* as well as the baby. It helps you to rediscover your own needs and desires; to express your feelings about the experience of having a child and what this does to your body; and to make realistic decisions about whether to have another child. It also includes women's moving accounts of their experiences of stillbirth and one mother's feelings about the challenge of caring for her handicapped child.

A sequel to BIRTH AND OUR BODIES, this essential post-natal companion guide is based on the author's successful classes and is organised for you to use alone, in pairs or in groups.

BIRTH AND OUR BODIES

Exercises and Meditations for the Childbearing Year and Preparation for Active Birth

Paddy O'Brien

This practical and positive companion guide provides women with detailed physical and mental exercises to practise through pregnancy and birth.

Working chronologically from the time when a woman may not even be pregnant but hopes to conceive in the near future, right through to the birth itself, the guide provides a comprehensive exercise programme for relaxation, combating morning sickness, stage fright in the last few weeks of pregnancy and for strengthening the pelvic floor muscles.

Illustrated with line drawings taken from 'life' both in the exercise classes which Paddy O'Brien runs, and at the time of the birth itself, BIRTH AND OUR BODIES helps mothers to stay in touch with a body, and in charge of it, when it seems in danger of being taken over by the baby. So, as well as maintaining and strengthening your muscles you get stronger and more supple emotionally.

This is a pocket-sized companion, easy to use at home, or at work — it encourages the participation of partners and can be used too whenever you have time to yourself.

'a gem, beautifully presented and designed, clear without being patronising.'

Helen Roberts

YOUR BODY, YOUR BABY, YOUR LIFE

Angela Phillips

with Nicky Lean and Barbara Jacobs

Your Body, Your Baby, Your Life starts with help on planning for pregnancy six months before you conceive, stays with you up to and through the birth and sees you safely into the world of new parenthood. It equips you with the information you need to work *with* health professionals, giving you a voice in your own care and allowing you to make decisions about the pregnancy and labour *you* want. It includes information on:

- choices in ante-natal treatment and the place of birth
- preparing yourself mentally and physically for childbirth
- recognising problems and assessing the help you are offered
- tests and their side effects
- understanding your rights and claiming benefits
- your body after pregnancy
- living with a new baby
- returning to work and much more!

'At last a book for the mother which regards her as a real person'
Anna Raeburn

'answers all those questions . . . you'd only dare ask your best friend. The horrors of feeling like a stranded whale, going off sex and wanting to cry all the time are all taken in the book's stride and Ros Asquith's cartoons don't let you forget the funny side of it all . . . it makes having a baby sound like fun, not an illness'
Company

'this baby book could be your best friend'
Mother Magazine

'A landmark in its field'
Jean Shapiro of *Good Housekeeping*

'Among the best pregnancy books we've ever seen'
Parents Magazine

THE TENTATIVE PREGNANCY

Prenatal Diagnosis and the Future of Motherhood

Barbara Katz Rothman

'Anyone who thinks that prenatal diagnosis is liberating for women should read this book.' – Ruth Hubbard, Harvard University.

More and more women are having children when they are over thirty and amniocentesis, primarily used as a test for Down's Syndrome, is becoming an automatic and routine part of prenatal care.

In this groundbreaking book, Barbara Katz Rothman draws on the experience of over 120 women and a wealth of expert testimony to show how one simple procedure can radically alter the way we think about childbirth and becoming a parent. The results of amniocentesis, and the more recently developed chorion villus sampling, force us to confront agonising dilemmas. What do you do if there is a 'problem' with the foetus? What kind of support can you expect if you decide to raise a handicapped child? How can you come to terms with the termination of a wanted pregnancy?

Passionate, sympathetic and at times heartbreaking, Barbara Katz Rothman's book is a must for anyone thinking of having a child.

'. . . makes women's experience of the technology visible for the first time . . . an immensely intelligent, sensitive and passionate book. No one can read it and remain unmoved.' – Gena Corea

'Wise, sensitive and disturbing – it should be obligatory reading for all health professionals working in this field, and for everyone who wants to understand the increasingly complex face of childbearing in today's world.' – Ann Oakley

0 86358 255 9

£5.95 pbk

A CHILD: YOUR CHOICE

Jean Shapiro

In the 1980's, we are often able to choose to be or not to be parents, but for today's women, the prospect of parenthood can be more daunting than ever before.

Recognising this dilemma, Jean Shapiro has written the book to help women who are undecided about having a baby. *A Child: Your Choice* is also for the woman who is pregnant and wants to consider the problems she might encounter after the birth of her child. This is *not* a Baby Book — it is a book about relationships between mothers and their partners, mothers and their children.

Basing her account firmly on quotations and interviews, Jean Shapiro presents a *realistic* appraisal of the difficulties faced by many parents. She describes the inevitable changes in lifestyle that having a child involves, the particular difficulties for working mothers and for those bringing up a child alone. Her book discusses important decisions such as the timing of pregnancy in relation to a woman's age and job, the choice of 'old' child versus two or more children, and the major questions of back-up support, of the implications of the AIDS virus, and of child-care options. She provides chapters on infertility and childlessness by choice, and the repercussions of these situations on the individual. Jean Shapiro's practical suggestions will help readers to overcome the many dilemmas that may make motherhood today such a challenge.

THE POLITICS OF BREASTFEEDING

Gabrielle Palmer

- As publicity about the benefits of breastfeeding increases, so too do the worldwide sales of artificial baby milk and feeding bottles
- Over-population and child malnutrition are the direct results of the decline in breastfeeding
- Every year, in the USA alone, 70,000 tons of tin plate are used up in discarded baby milk tins
- For the first time in recorded history, the impotent female breast has become a mass sexual fetish

Gabrielle Palmer's powerful and provocative book shows that breastfeeding is much more than a matter of personal inclination. Women all over the world are being pressurised into feeding their babies artificially and this affects us all: our health, our environment and the global economy.

Gabrielle Palmer questions whether bottlefeeding really frees women to lead more fulfilling lives, and examines social attitudes in a world where a woman who does breastfeed her child risks losing what little income she earns. She traces the commercial reasons behind medical recommendations, and alerts us to basic nutritional facts and the controversy over breastfeeding in the light of AIDS, radiation and breast cancer.

0 86358 219 2

£5.95 pbk